INVESTING

IN

MUNICIPAL
BONDS

INVESTING

IN

MUNICIPAL
BONDS

How to Balance
Risk and Reward for Success
in Today's Bond Market

PHILIP FISCHER

New York   Chicago   San Francisco   Lisbon   London   Madrid   Mexico City
Milan   New Delhi   San Juan   Seoul   Singapore   Sydney   Toronto

This publication is designed to provide accurate and authoritative information in regard to the subject matter covered. It is sold with the understanding that the publisher is not engaged in rendering legal, accounting, securities trading, or other professional services. If legal advice or other expert assistance is required, the services of a competent professional person should be sought.

> —*From a Declaration of Principles Jointly Adopted by a Committee of the American Bar Association and a Committee of Publishers and Associations*

Figure credits and table credits are listed as sources in the captions under the affected figures and tables. They are also listed in the References Section on pp. 239–253.

McGraw-Hill books are available at special quantity discounts to use as premiums and sales promotions or for use in corporate training programs. To contact a representative, please e-mail us at bulksales@mcgraw-hill.com.

This book is printed on acid-free paper.

For my wife

Contents

Preface

This book is designed to help investors, issuers, and regulators come to terms with the changes that are taking place in the municipal bond market. Having worked with participants in the market for decades, I believe there's a need for a better understanding of the function and functioning of municipal bonds. The use of the municipal bond market to allow taxpayers to "pay as they use" public projects is an essential tool for state and local governments. The way in which the municipal bond market operates, however, has changed dramatically over the last several years with the introduction of new forms of taxable municipal bonds and the demise of the auction-rate market and a number of bond insurers.

This book is designed to offer a practical approach to the municipal bond market—an approach that lies somewhere between financial theory and the minutiae of bond calculations. A little of both is required.

This has been a tempestuous couple of years in the municipal bond industry, and the municipal market today is far different from what it was when I began studying municipal bonds in the 1970s. Then the municipal bond market was smaller, simpler, and often disregarded. The world is different now, and governmental markets are seen as the backbones of finance.

Governmental markets—particularly the U.S. municipal bond market—have contributed mightily to the growth of the nation, yet they continue to be the subject of continuous tinkering and criticism from our political establishment.

Some improvement is always possible, and no market has performed perfectly in the last several years. That said, the government officials who are criticizing the market are often the least likely to improve it.

Micromanaging market processes to achieve social distributions can significantly inhibit the functioning of a market, to the detriment of all. Traditionally, the municipal market has enhanced private-market development through investments in public infrastructure and education. In the future, we can expect that this market will be just as essential, even as infrastructure becomes more ethereal. The municipal bond market will continue to play a critical role in developing the digital and physical highways of the future.

Acknowledgments

This book is the realization of many years of studying and practicing public finance. It began with my fine professors at the University of Oregon, where my first academic studies were on the structure of the municipal bond market. Later my colleagues at Citi, Salomon Brothers, and especially Merrill Lynch helped me understand the practical side of the business. I am also grateful to John Sprung and others for their helpful comments on the book.

In addition, I would like to thank the British Bankers' Association (BBA); Bank for International Settlements (BIS); Bloomberg L.P.; Daniel Bergstresser, Associate Professor of Finance, Brandeis International Business School; Financial Industry Regulatory Authority (FINRA); Fitch Ratings; Moody's Investors Service; Municipal Securities Rulemaking Board (MSRB); *The Bond Buyer*; Thomson Reuters Municipal Market Data (MMD); and the Securities Industry and Financial Markets Association (SIFMA) for allowing the use of their materials.

INVESTING

IN

MUNICIPAL
BONDS

1

A Little History

America is a country that was formed by putting together a number of pieces. As the states came together, they gave—often grudgingly—the central government the powers it needed in order to operate. Of course, a lot has changed since the republic was formed, but understanding the basic outline of how the municipal bond market was created will tell us a great deal about what it looks like now and where it's going. Unlike corporations, which are actually formed by states, the states themselves don't go away when times get tough. And neither do their bonds.

MONEY, MONEY

When they came to America, the colonists didn't bring banks with them—nor did they bring much money, for that matter. The metal needed to make silver and gold coins was especially hard to come by in the colonies. Necessity, though, is the mother of invention. On December 10, 1690, the colony of Massachusetts was financially broke and facing rebellion by its soldiers, who had been sent on an expedition against the French in Canada. The colony expected that it could use booty taken in the campaign to pay the troops. Unfortunately, things did not turn out well militarily, but the troops still needed to be paid. The General Assembly came to the rescue by authorizing the printing of paper money for the colonial treasury.

Good ideas are rarely wasted. New Hampshire, Rhode Island, Connecticut, New York, and New Jersey authorized the printing of paper money in 1711. South Carolina (1712), Pennsylvania (1723), Maryland (1734), Delaware (1739), Virginia (1755), and Georgia (1760) then followed suit.

Of course, things quickly went out of control as the colonies printed more and more paper money. A wide variety of colonial paper money existed, some bearing interest and some not. Some was legal tender or was legal tender only when paid to the colony. In some cases, the devaluation created from printing so much paper was quite severe. For example, Rhode Island's currency depreciated by 96 percent in just a few years as a result of excess printing.

The colonies also fought to protect the market for their currency by passing laws to prevent the circulation of the other colonies' paper within their borders. Finally, in 1774, the English largely banned the use of colonial paper. These lessons weren't lost on the framers of the U.S. Constitution. Congress is explicitly given the authority "to coin Money, regulate the Value thereof," and the states are expressly prohibited from having their own monetary system: "No State shall ... coin Money; emit Bills of Credit; make any Thing but gold and silver Coin a Tender in Payment of Debts."

With the signing of the Constitution, the large debts incurred by the states during the Revolutionary War were assumed by Congress: "All Debts contracted and Engagements entered into, before the Adoption of this Constitution, shall be as valid against the United States under this Constitution, as under the Confederation."

Yet while the states gave up their power to print money, they did not give up the ability to borrow money. It is this capacity to borrow that lies at the heart of the municipal bond market.

Bear in mind that it is the states, and only the states, that have the inherent right to borrow. States engage in borrowing for a myriad of purposes. In addition, however, the states can, and often do, grant their political and economic entities—counties, cities, authorities, special districts, and so on—the authority to issue debt under certain circumstances. The states frequently specify the maximum amount that their political subdivisions can borrow, the method of repayment, what the borrowed money can be used for (the use of proceeds), and a myriad of other details.

The Constitution has this to say about the states' use of their borrowing authority: "No person shall ... be deprived of life, liberty, or property, without due process of law; nor shall private property be taken for public use, without just compensation."

What constitutes "due process" changes with the context, but in general, the government can levy taxes or take property only for public purposes. (*Public purposes* is itself a term of art, and it can sometimes be broadly defined.) In addition, when property is taken, the owners must be fairly compensated.

Rights created by contract are a form of property and are subject to public taking, which means that a state is not forever bound by the terms of a bond contract. On the other hand, if the state acts to alter the contract to the disadvantage of the bondholder, it is obliged to fairly compensate the other party. However, if the state's actions don't harm the bondholder, or do so in only a minor way, the courts will be reluctant to intervene.

States are also constitutionally required to observe their contracts. The "contract clause" in the Constitution specifies that no state may pass a "Law impairing the Obligation of Contracts." Without this contract clause, bondholders would have to confront the general rule that one legislature cannot bind succeeding legislatures. This is logical; otherwise, we would still be living under Puritan laws from the seventeenth century. But when the legislature's intent is clearly to impair the value of an investor's rights, a court can force the state to observe its original agreement without regard to subsequent laws.

DEFAULTS ON OBLIGATIONS ARE NOT BANKRUPTCIES

States and local governments cannot simply ignore their debt obligations. Nevertheless, a lender to a state, like any lender, faces the possibility that the borrower could suffer financial difficulties and be unable to pay what is due on time.

Defaults on municipal bonds are unusual but not unheard of. It is important to understand, though, that a default is not a bankruptcy.

Defaults occur when an agreement in the bond contract is not met. These failures to meet an agreement are divided roughly into monetary defaults, which are serious, and others, which are technical. A monetary default is the failure to make a payment on time. The payment can be an interest payment or a principal payment. Usually it has to be overdue by a fixed period of time, such as 30 days, to be considered a default, but any missed payment can immediately have very serious consequences.

A technical default is any nonmonetary default. These could include the failure to maintain the property built with the loan in an agreed-upon manner, the failure to keep reserve or other funds at a specified level, or the failure to submit reports to the lender within a fixed period of time.

The important thing is that a default can be cured or fixed. Usually the lender and the borrower work things out; if they do not, the parties will usually resort to a judicial procedure, such as appealing to a federal judge in bankruptcy to supervise the process of the lender and the borrowers' coming to terms.

STATE AND LOCAL GOVERNMENT BORROWING

Even at this early point in the book, it is important to note that state and local governments have, in general, been very responsible borrowers. Access to the capital markets is a key element of public policy. One of a government's more important jobs is to borrow money to pay for capital projects. In theory, a state can merely save up the tax payments it receives to build a public facility like a highway. However, these projects are expensive. Using a "pay-as-you-go" approach like this means that a large amount of money ends up sitting in the government's bank account, which can create political problems.

Suppose, for instance, that the state wants to build a road. If the road is in the western part of the state, the residents of the eastern sector may not think it fair. In addition, unions and others may seek to divert some of the money to other purposes that they deem worthy. And taxpayers know that public funds have a way of walking, and so they resist being taxed to enable the state to accumulate a lot of money. Also, the capital project often has a longer life than most taxpayers, so the current residents may not want to fund the next generation's needs.

Borrowing the capital to build an asset like the road is often the preferred approach. This is a "pay-as-you-use" method in which the actual users pay for the road as they use it. A pay-as-you-use method also provides an equitable solution for mobile populations. The current taxpayers usually don't want to be taxed to benefit outsiders. Cities and states that have taxed themselves heavily to provide facilities and services can find themselves a destination for out-of-state migrants from poorer areas who are attracted by the better infrastructure. Even without more facilities and services, some states will naturally be a magnet for immigration, imposing costs on the current residents.

The law is clear that a state must admit Americans from other states. This was made poignantly clear in the

Depression-era Okie cases. During the Dust Bowl, indigents who had been forced off their farms in hard-hit states like Oklahoma often headed to California. However, when they arrived, they were frequently either turned away at the state border or arrested. And anyone who brought the poor into the state was also liable. Consider California's anti-Okie law:

> *Every person, firm or corporation, or officer or agent thereof that brings or assists in bringing into the State any indigent person who is not a resident of the State, knowing him to be an indigent person, is guilty of a misdemeanor.*

The U.S. Supreme Court invalidated the law and made it clear that "poverty and immorality are not synonymous."

Citizens of the United States can live wherever they want in this country. As noble as this policy is, it is not without its consequences for public finance. Pay-as-you-use is a critical tool for handling the impact on infrastructure and taxes that migratory populations create. However, pay-as-you-use requires access to capital markets, and that, in turn, requires the borrower to be creditworthy. This is a point that is well understood at the state level.

RATINGS ARE A GOOD GUIDE
FOR CREDIT WORTHINESS

Moody's Investors Service, one of the oldest bond-rating firms, gives a good picture of the creditworthiness of municipal borrowers. Over the years, it has produced studies examining the performance of bonds rated by the firm. In a recent study, Moody's sampled the period from 1970 to 2011. The sample contained 1,500 ratings in 1970, which expanded to about 17,700 in 2011.

Over the course of this 41 years, Moody's reported 71 monetary defaults in which the issuer failed to pay interest or principal. Other studies define defaults somewhat differently, including occasions when the issuer drew funds from a reserve account, for example. But it is a monetary default that investors would be most concerned about. Bonds that were not rated defaulted more frequently, but these nonrated bonds constitute a small part of the market and investors can avoid most of the default risk in the market by merely buying rated bonds.

Of course, in periods of financial stress, municipal issuers are likely to experience problems with tax revenues, but this tends to happen with a lag. During recessionary periods, their revenues decline, even after the recession is over. Moody's reported that in 2010 and 2011, after the Great Recession had officially ended, defaults rose to 5.5 per year, whereas the average number of defaults from 1970 to 2009 was 1.5 per year.

Municipal bond defaults also tend to be concentrated in a few types of bonds. Healthcare- and housing-related borrowing had the most defaults, 73 percent of the total. Still, the numbers are not huge for rated bonds: 29 defaults for housing and 23 for hospitals.

The bonds sold by cities, counties, and other state subdivisions that were repayable from the taxes of the issuer rarely defaulted and constituted only 7 percent of the sample's defaults.

If an issuer has problems, the lender's difficulties don't end there. The ultimate recovery in a default usually involves a return of some or all of the principal. With municipal bonds, the average recovery is around 65 percent of principal, although it varies greatly by the type of bond, and it may take some time to get the money returned. With corporate bonds, it is about 49 percent.

These results are for rated bonds and are generally consistent with the findings of other rating agencies when they examine the defaults on the bonds they rate. However, the issuer pays for the rating, and as a result many bonds are not rated—either because it is not economical to pay for a rating for a small issue or because the issuer would not like the rating it would receive. For investors who lack either the expertise or the time to keep track of an issuer's creditworthiness, the advice is generally either to buy rated bonds and keep track of the ratings, or to have the bonds professionally managed by a fund manager.

Municipal bond raters have had a relatively good record. Ratings of municipal bonds have been more reliable than those of taxable bonds, although the history of ratings for municipal bond insurance companies is difficult to defend. Municipal bond rating is a specialized segment of the bond rating industry and has shown itself to be far more accurate than mortgage bond rating, for example. Municipal bond ratings have been a useful guide for investors, although, as we will see, the standards for selecting the rating grade have been recalibrated in recent years to be more consistent with the scale used for corporate bonds.

No one is perfect, though, and the overriding rule is not to keep all of one's eggs in one basket. Diversification, even in relatively safe instruments, is always the best advice.

MUNICIPAL BANKRUPTCY

States are sovereigns, and lending to sovereigns is a problem because they can control the rules of the game by refusing to be sued, restricting suits to their own terms, or limiting the time within which a legal claim can be filed. In addition, both the nature of the claim and the amount of the damages can be limited. However, the constitutional reassurances discussed earlier give investors some comfort that the states and localities cannot merely legislate their way out of their debts.

All of that is fine, but what happens if the state or local government simply runs out of money, and the issuer and the lenders cannot agree on a resolution? In that case, a lender may seek help in court. One of the oldest remedies for forcing a governmental body to pay what it owes is a mandamus action. In general, such an action does what it sounds like: the court mandates that the officials of a governmental unit do what they are supposed to do under the agreement. Its use is often written into the documents of the lending agreement. Here is some sample language from a lease agreement:

> *Lessor must first seek through a mandamus action to enforce the payment of the Rent Payments due hereunder by the levying of ad valorem taxes, without limit as to rate or amount.*

In other words, the person who is leasing the property, the lessor, has to go to court and ask the court to compel the governmental unit to make the payments due on the lease by increasing property (ad valorem) taxes as much as necessary.

Mandamus suits in municipal bonds have a long and checkered history. In the Reconstruction of the South after the Civil War, the administrators from the North were often highly unscrupulous in their issuance of municipal debt. The citizens were so incensed that they refused to make payments on the bonds. They didn't just default; they repudiated the bonds, saying that their issuance was null and void in the first case. Mandamus suits by out-of-state bondholders were of limited value when the court sought to compel local officials to pay and a different mayor showed up each day.

Mandamus is basically a state court remedy. There is now also a federal remedy allowing lenders to recover damages, but the lenders' rights are limited. The U.S. Constitution specifically authorizes Congress "to establish . . . uniform Laws on the subject of Bankruptcies throughout the United States." Because the Constitution grants the authority to create bankruptcy provisions to Congress, states are preempted in this area and can't have their own conflicting bankruptcy laws. The U.S. Constitution is the law of the land. When the Constitution grants Congress power to act, no state law can overrule it. And Congress is empowered to pass bankruptcy laws.

Congress has used this authority to create an extensive legal system to help debtors and creditors in times of crisis. Most people are familiar with its basic elements. The Bankruptcy Code (Title 11 of the U.S. Code) is broken down into chapters. The three that usually come to mind are those that generally apply to wage earners (Chapter 13 of the code), corporate reorganizations (Chapter 11), and liquidations of individual and corporate property to pay creditors (Chapter 7).

State and local governments are not covered by these provisions. In fact, the states themselves are not authorized to file for bankruptcy. There have been proposals that the states be allowed to file for bankruptcy, but that is widely regarded as bad policy. The mere existence of a right to file for bankruptcy would introduce a new and very serious risk for municipal bondholders, who would demand to be compensated for it. The compensation would show up as higher borrowing costs for the states and for local governments. As a result, the states themselves have campaigned against allowing states to file for bankruptcy.

In addition to states not being allowed to file for bankruptcy, the contract clause prohibits states from legislating their way out of problems with their debts and the debts of their subdivisions. Thus, when a city is in financial trouble, the state cannot simply pass a law invalidating the city's debts.

Normally, bankruptcy proceedings for local governments are not a significant issue, since very few of these entities actually need them. The Great Depression, however, created such dire economic circumstances that Congress created a provision in the Bankruptcy Code to help cities, counties, and other units of local government manage their debt problems. During the Depression, there were situations in which a municipality would seek a mutual agreement among all of its creditors for a specific remedy or a payment schedule, but one or more creditors would hold out for a better deal. Neither the state nor the municipality could force the creditors into an agreement because of the limitations they had under the contract clause. Congress deemed that some form of federal remedy was needed; thus Chapter 9 of the Bankruptcy Code was created.

Municipal Bankruptcy—An Investor's Perspective

Here we give an overview of the general features of municipal bankruptcy from an investor's perspective. Like the other legal discussions presented in this book, it is not and cannot be exhaustive. Recourse to expert tax and legal advice on specific issues is always recommended.

The laws created for municipalities in Chapter 9 of the Bankruptcy Code presented Congress with a unique set of challenges, partly because of their scope. The law applied to "municipalities"; however, the term included both the political subdivisions of a state as well as state agencies and other authorities providing public services.

In applying the Bankruptcy Code to political subdivisions of states, Congress is confronted with severe limitations. Congress cannot take over the political authority of the states. The Tenth Amendment to the Constitution embeds in our laws the idea that the powers of Congress are limited to those given to it in the Constitution, and that no general authority beyond that can be assumed. For states, a residual "police power" exists: "The powers not delegated to the United States by the Constitution, nor prohibited by it to the States, are reserved to the States respectively, or to the people."

Congress must respect the existence and power of the states. It cannot use its authority to legislate a Bankruptcy Code in such a way as to significantly diminish the states' authority over their units of local government. A municipality, for example, must be specifically authorized by the state to file for federal bankruptcy. Silence on the part of the state does not mean that it has implicitly consented to the municipality's filing for bankruptcy. The state can explicitly deny the municipality the authority to seek bankruptcy protection. If the state wished to, it could compel one of its municipalities to file for bankruptcy.

Municipal Bankruptcy Law

There are many tricky areas in municipal bankruptcy law. In addition to the federal government respecting a state's authority, a state must respect the authority of Congress. If one of its municipalities has filed for bankruptcy, the state cannot choose which parts of the Bankruptcy Code it would like to have applied to the municipality. Yet even with that limitation on state conduct, the state exercises a great deal of control over a municipality when that municipality is in bankruptcy.

Unlike the situation with a corporate bankruptcy, the creditors in a municipal bankruptcy cannot force the municipality into court. There are no involuntary municipal bankruptcies. The creditors cannot force a court-appointed trustee on a municipality or submit a plan for reorganization.

The municipality is not entirely free to act as it wishes, though. A municipality must act in good faith before the bankruptcy court will accept the case. For a municipality to prove that it has acted in good faith, it must show that it has negotiated in good faith with its creditors. The clearest way to show good faith is to get the consent of a majority of the creditors to filing for bankruptcy, although that is not required. For bondholders, bonds secured by specific revenue streams are superior in priority to unsecured claims in terms of their access to the assets of the municipality. They get paid ahead of unsecured claims. Thus, for example, if the issuer were to go into bankruptcy, a water and sewer bond secured by revenue from a water authority may have its principal and interest paid before a general obligation bond. Revenue bonds retain their secured status in bankruptcy and so cannot be converted into general obligation bonds.

When the municipal entity is subject to federal bankruptcy court, the court cannot interdict any of the political or governmental powers of the municipality. Nor can it intervene with regard to any of the municipality's property or revenues.

While it can be difficult to navigate, Chapter 9 of the Bankruptcy Code gives local governments three important benefits. First, it provides an automatic stay, which prohibits creditors from suing to recover what is owed them for a time. Second, a bankruptcy proceeding creates a bankruptcy plan that provides a process for repaying a municipality's debts. Finally, bankruptcy gives the court the power to reject union collective bargaining agreements. The last benefit, rejecting union agreements, is much more restricted for corporations in a Chapter 11 bankruptcy than it is for municipalities in Chapter 9. Corporations must negotiate with unions when altering labor agreements in bankruptcy. Municipalities, with the help of the court, can effectively change these agreements unilaterally.

Investors need to realize that in spite of the benefits of municipal bankruptcy very few cases have been filed. Most of the filings have come from California, Texas, and Nebraska. In total, there have been only about 600 cases since the depths of the Great Depression. In part, this is because a minority of the states have authorized the use of municipal bankruptcy. By 2010, nineteen states had authorized their subdivisions to file for federal bankruptcy.

EFFECTS OF 2007–2008 CRISIS ON MUNICIPAL BOND MARKET

The financial crisis of 2007–2008 created a chaotic environment in the bond markets. And while it did not lead to extensive defaults in the municipal bond market, the basic sequence of events should be understood in order to appreciate the radical restructuring of the municipal bond market that occurred at that time.

On February 27, 2007, the Federal Home Loan Mortgage Corporation (Freddie Mac) stopped its purchases of risky subprime mortgages and mortgage-related securities. In April, a large subprime lender filed for Chapter 11 bankruptcy. On June 1, Standard & Poor's (S&P) and Moody's downgraded a group of subprime mortgage–backed bonds. This was followed by further downgrades by rating agencies, mortgage hedge fund liquidations, and more mortgage lender bankruptcies. By August 2007, the Fed noted that banks were having problems meeting their funding needs because of problems in the money and credit markets. Countrywide Financial Corporation was downgraded and borrowed all of its available credits—$11.5 billion. The financial markets were in turmoil, and the Federal Open Market Committee of the Federal Reserve (the Fed) began aggressively cutting short-term rates.

In December 2007, the Fed created the Term Auction Facility (TAF) to lend funds to banks. The loans were secured by various types of collateral. Currency swap lines were created by the Fed for the European Central Bank and the Swiss National Bank.

On January 11, 2008, Bank of America announced its purchase of Countrywide Financial for $4 billion. A week later, Fitch downgraded Ambac Financial Group's insurance rating to AA. This was the beginning of Armageddon for the monoline insurers (so called because they are restricted to offering a single type or line of insurance).

In the meantime, the municipal bond market received a number of other shocks. One of the greatest shocks to the municipal market during the credit debacle was the end of the $330 billion auction-rate securities market. In this market, long-term bonds and preferred stock were financed at low short-term rates.

With these securities, the issuer received the benefit of using a short-term instrument's lower yield. Typically, if the security was auctioned every seven days, the issuer received the seven-day interest rate. It did not have rollover risk—the risk that it might need to sell a new bond to pay off the old one every seven days—because the instrument had a long-term maturity. On the other hand, each auction needed to "clear." That is, in an auction, every last dollar of a bond that was auctioned needed to be sold to someone, and there were thousands of auctions among the various dealers on Wall Street.

This market had existed for decades with very few "fails," or auctions that did not sell all the bonds. The small number of fails was a consequence of the bonds being of high credit quality—typically because of bank backing through letters of credit or other types of credit support. And it is now clear that when the last dollar was needed in an auction, the money often came from the bank that was running the auction.

In February 2008, banks stopped supporting the auctions by supplying their own capital. The result was an immediate collapse of the auction-rate market. There was a run on the market and panic selling.

In March 2008, the Carlyle Capital Corporation failed to meet margin calls, and its mortgage bond fund defaulted. The Fed created a series of lending vehicles for banks and expanded its swap lines.

In June 2008, Standard & Poor's downgraded Ambac and MBIA from AAA to AA. On July 15, the SEC gave an emergency order halting naked short selling of Fannie Mae and Freddie Mac, as well as of large banks and investment banks. On September 7, 2008, Fannie Mae and Freddie Mac were put in government receivership. In addition, Bank of America issued a press release stating that it would acquire Merrill Lynch & Co. for $50 billion in mid-September. And on September 15, Lehman Brothers filed for Chapter 11 bankruptcy.

At this point, the municipal bond market had seen a substantial amount of volatility, but the coup de grâce came

with the further downgrades of the bond insurance companies. These insurance companies dated from the 1970s. The
first company, Ambac, was formed in 1971 and was followed a few years later by the Municipal Bond Insurance
Association (MBIA). The business was slow to develop,
since very few municipal bonds defaulted. Acceptance of
insurance grew, however, with the default of New York City
in 1975 and the Washington Public Power Supply System
(or WPPSS, pronounced "whoops") in 1983. In 2003,
slightly less than half of all new issues were insured. This
had expanded to about 57 percent by 2005.

A list of insurers at that time included:

- Ambac Assurance Corporation
- American Overseas Reinsurance Company Limited
- Assured Guaranty Corp. (AGC)
- Assured Guaranty Municipal (AGM)
- CIFG
- Financial Guaranty Insurance Company (FGIC)
- MBIA Inc.
- National Public Finance Guarantee
- Radian
- Syncora Guarantee, Inc.

Even as business accelerated, the investment and insurance
patterns of the insurers changed, moving away from insuring
municipal bonds to insuring derivatives, particularly mortgage
derivatives like collateralized debt obligations (CDOs), which
are pools of loans or mortgages. The fall of the mortgage and
derivatives markets in 2008 led directly to the demise of the
insurance companies. By 2011, insurance penetration had

Table 1-1   S&P Monoline Insurers' Ratings

Month	Year	Ambac	Assured	CIFG	FGIC	FSA	MBIA	XL Capital
September	2009	CC	AAA	CC	CC	AAA	BB+	R
December	2008	A	AAA	B	CCC	AAA	AA	B
December	2007	AAA	AAA	AAA	AAA	AAA	AAA	AAA
December	2006	AAA	AAA	AAA	AAA	AAA	AAA	AAA
December	2005	AAA	AAA	AAA	AAA	AAA	AAA	AAA
December	2004	AAA	AAA	AAA	AAA	AAA	AAA	AAA

Source: Siddharth Bhaskar Shenai et al., "Financial Guarantors and the 2007–2009 Credit Crisis," AFA 2011 Denver Meetings Paper, March 15, 2010, Table 4.

collapsed to 5 percent of total new issuance. Table 1-1 shows the rapid collapse of some of the larger insurers' ratings.

Not all insurers became equally encumbered. FSA and Assured Guaranty were less affected than some of the others. In addition, Berkshire Hathaway created a monoline insurer in 2008, reaping the benefits created by the problems of the other monoline insurers. This firm insured bonds at a substantial premium when it entered the market in 2008, but it was active only for a limited time.

The loss of the insurers' AAA ratings did not lead to a widespread wave of defaults, as some had feared. For the most part, the insurers used a zero-loss standard; that is, the losses they expected to realize on their insurance policies were zero. They would write policies only on issues that probably should have been AAA anyway. Because the municipal rating scale used at the time was systematically lower than the corporate scale, the corporate insurer was AAA, but a municipal bond that the insurer viewed as essentially default-free was often rated AA or A. The lower-rated municipal bond received the insurer's AAA when the issuer bought the insurance and the rating agency rerated the bond.

Recalibration of the ratings has largely corrected this, as we will see in Chapter 4, but the difference in rating methods drove the insurance business for many years. That insured bonds rarely needed insurance became apparent when the insurers lost their AAA ratings. Most insured bonds already had an underlying rating, even though the bond was traded at the insurer's rating. The insurance provided a "wrap." When the insurers' ratings fell, those bonds that did not have an underlying rating became relatively illiquid.

Not only did the problems with the insurance companies reduce the number of new insured municipal bonds, but the basic pricing of insured bonds also changed. Prior to 2007, insured municipal bonds were generally rated AAA and priced accordingly. They were some of the most expensive bonds and were sought after, especially on derivatives desks. Now, it is not unusual for insured bonds to trade at lower prices than noninsured bonds. In fact, this is an area where investors should look for value. The investors, however, should understand that some of the insurance companies may not in fact be capable of paying in the event that the underlying issuer defaults. In addition, bond insurers have often received negative press, giving them a kind of headline risk. The change in the credit status of insured bonds has also made them less liquid than many other bonds, especially if they lack an underlying rating.

The municipal bond market did not entirely escape the chaotic situation confronting the stock and bond markets worldwide. That having been said, with the clarity of hindsight, we can see that there were clues to the problems that were to come. In the thick of it, though, exactly what would transpire in the market was far from certain. However, we can now say that, on the whole, the municipal market survived its greatest stress test since the Great Depression without the often predicted wave of mass defaults. It is a lesson about the resilience of this market.

The practical consequences of defaults and bankruptcy vastly outweigh the legal benefits. The 2011 *New York Times Magazine* article "Broke Town" surveys the city of Vallejo, California, following its bankruptcy and provides a good synopsis of what happened to a city whose decay was only exacerbated by bankruptcy. At its core, a city that is in bankruptcy may well expect to find city services severely impaired and access to credit, which is essential to maintaining its infrastructure, cut off. As the *New York Times* piece notes, "the fantasy of using bankruptcy to suspend government runs up against a hard truth: even in bankruptcy, cities and states don't disappear—nor do their obligations."

If what happened in Vallejo is not dramatic enough, the experience of New York City in 1975 is even more enlightening. The city had a technical default on a note that delayed a payment for a few days. The net result was the installation of a state control board to oversee city finances for a decade. City officials were forced to make a humiliating appearance in Washington, DC, asking the federal government for assistance when the state refused to help. While there is a great deal of controversy around the details, it's hard to forget the *Daily News* headline from October 30, 1975: "Ford to City: Drop Dead." New York City was effectively barred from the bond markets for eight years and was not able to borrow in its own name during that time. The net effect was a significant reduction in the quality of life in the city as its infrastructure deteriorated.

TYPES OF GOVERNMENT UNITS THAT ISSUE BONDS

Here it is important to point out that the municipal bond market supports the economic activities of tens of thousands of governmental units; see Table 1-2 for a breakdown. These include counties, municipalities, townships, school districts, and the largest single category, special districts. Special districts are specially created entities that are designed to provide a specific service, such as transportation. In theory, then, each of these states and local units of government is able to borrow money and thus issue municipal bonds.

These public entities encompass virtually every type of legal activity. Investors of all types lend money to support these enterprises. The municipal bond market is a very

Table 1-2   Type of Government, 1997

Total		87,504
U.S. government		1
State government		50
Local governments		87,453
County governments	3,043	
Municipal governments	19,372	
Township and town governments	16,629	
School districts	13,726	
Special districts	34,683	

Source: U.S. Census Bureau.

high-grade market with few defaults, but it is not and cannot be risk free. Some activities are inherently risky. For example, a housing development district selling tax increment bonds to build the roads, lights, and other infrastructure for a new housing development has some inherent risk to it. As we have seen with the recent housing bust, if the housing development is not completed, the incremental new taxes that the district was going to use to repay the bonds will not materialize, and the bonds may default.

For most investors, the rule is straightforward: know what you are buying. If the risk is not appropriate, don't lend the money. There are many kinds of issuers and investors, however. The muni market can and should allow for the limited use of risk capital to build speculative projects. That said, disclosure of the speculative nature of these projects is mandatory.

2

A First Look at Municipal Bonds

Having talked about the power of the states to borrow money, let's move on to some examples. We will be making use of data from the Municipal Securities Rulemaking Board (MSRB). The MSRB was created during the market chaos of 1975 and since then has seen a steady expansion of its authority. The Securities and Exchange Commission (SEC) oversees the MSRB, approving and enforcing the MSRB rules. The MSRB is one of several regulatory agencies charged with promoting a well-functioning market and preventing fraud and manipulation. It maintains a body of investor protection and other municipal market rules designed to do just that.

Municipal Bond Acronyms

SEC   Securities and Exchange Commission
        Regulates the national securities and markets

MSRB Municipal Securities Rulemaking Board
        Establishes rules for the municipal market

FINRA	Financial Industry Regulatory Authority
	Regulates brokerage firms
SIFMA	Securities Industry and Financial Markets Association
	Operates as an industry trade group
EMMA	MSRB's Electronic Municipal Market Access website
	Reports on municipal bond trades

The Financial Industry Regulatory Authority (FINRA) regulates all securities firms doing business in the United States. FINRA is responsible for around 4,400 brokerage firms and around 630,000 registered securities representatives. It provides an extensive amount of information on the securities markets for the public. FINRA is also the enforcement arm of the MSRB with respect to municipal bonds. The Securities Industry and Financial Markets Association (SIFMA), an industry trade group representing the large banks, asset managers, and other major securities firms, also provides a wealth of information for investors.

States and local governments are exempt from many of the provisions of the federal securities laws. For example, there are no prospectuses, as there are with corporate bonds. However, the antifraud provisions of the federal securities laws do apply. Fraud in municipal transactions is prohibited, and materially false statements are banned.

The rules are extensive, but it is worth pointing out a few of the more important ones. These govern the behavior of certain key market participants: brokers and dealers. Brokers, as the term implies, stand between the buyer of a bond and somebody else. The other party may be an individual or an institution. The broker earns a fee for its effort, called a commission.

A dealer, on the other hand, buys and sells bonds for itself and maintains an inventory. It is the dealer who is the market maker. The dealer literally makes the market go. As payment for its services, the dealer buys low and sells high. The difference between the price paid for the bond and the sales price is the bid-asked spread. The dealer pays the bid price or bid side and sells at the asked price. Since securities firms usually provide both broker and dealer services, they are referred to as broker/dealers.

Brokers and dealers are subject to stringent rules and have to meet strict professional standards. These are not usually academic qualifications. One doesn't need an MBA to be a broker, but the MSRB has established a series of professional examinations specific to the individual's functions, which are growing in number and complexity.

SAMPLE RULES OF THE MSRB

The MSRB has established rules in a number of areas, a few of which are discussed here.

Recordkeeping

Brokers and dealers are required to observe detailed rules about recordkeeping. The content, location, and timing of financial records are specified. In some cases, surprise audits are required, at the dealer's expense.

How Trades Take Place

How trades take place is also carefully governed. The contract for the purchase or sale of a bond is established on the trade date. The money and the securities are exchanged on the settlement date. On the settlement date, the buyer and the seller settle up.

For municipal bonds, the settlement date is usually three days after the trade date. If this is the case, the trade is said to be done *regular way* and is referred to as T+3 or the trade date plus three days. Trading conventions vary for different markets. For example, regular way for Treasury bonds is T+1. There are many different trading conventions for different instruments and situations.

Spot and Forward Markets

Securities that trade in the regular way are said to be in the *spot market*. There is a *forward market* as well. A bond sale may take place on February 1, but the settlement may not occur until three months later. This type of forward sale is common in most financial markets. The MSRB provides formulas for the calculation of prices and the timing of payments for the bonds in such situations.

Underwriting Regulations

Scandals in the early 1990s involving New Jersey Turnpike Authority bonds and others led to an expansion of the MSRB's underwriting regulations. Underwriting is the process of buying the entire bond issue from the public entity and selling off the bonds in smaller pieces. The broker/dealer will buy low from the issuer and sell high to retail and institutional customers. The difference between the amount paid to the issuer and that earned in selling the bonds is the *underwriting spread*.

Pay to Play

One thing that cannot be done is "pay to play." Paying to play was a practice in which a broker/dealer paid government officials to be able to underwrite their bonds. Pay to play was a corrupt way of buying the new issue spread because the issuer was not necessarily getting the highest price for the bonds. Pay to play is now banned. Underwriters cannot bribe the issuer's officials with gifts or gratuities, either directly or through the use of consultants or lobbyists.

Disclosures

Investors and professionals in the municipal bond market are also barred by the SEC from "deceptive, dishonest, or unfair practices." What this means varies with the circumstances. The underwriter is required to make a series of disclosures to the issuer. These include telling the issuer that:

- The MSRB requires that issuers and investors be dealt with fairly at all times.
- The underwriting transaction is arm's length.
- The underwriter is not a fiduciary of the issuer and so isn't required to act in the issuer's best interest at all times.

- The price paid for the issuer's bonds must be fair and reasonable.
- Underwriters have responsibilities for disclosures made by the issuer to investors.

A dealer's responsibility to make fair disclosures continues after it has bought the bonds from the issuer. The MSRB rules require that a dealer disclose to the customer all material information that the dealer knows about the bonds. This includes "material information" that the dealer could reasonably get from established industry sources like Reuters, Bloomberg, and other data providers. These sources are expensive, and it is unlikely that individuals would have access to them.

Information is material if not disclosing it would change the total mix of information available to the customer. Certainly, a dealer who is selling a municipal bond needs to give the customer a complete description of the security so that a reasonable investor can identify potential risks associated with it.

Sophisticated Municipal Market Professional

Different customers have different levels of sophistication, and institutions are expected to know more than the typical retail customer. When a dealer is trading with a "sophisticated municipal market professional," or SMMP, it must still act fairly, but knowing widely available industry information is generally the responsibility of the SMMP.

SMMPs are institutional and high-net-worth customers of dealers. These customers include:

- A bank, savings and loan association, insurance company, or registered investment company
- An investment advisor
- Any other entity with at least $50 million

A customer that is not an SMMP is a retail customer, and the dealer has higher standards of disclosure.

Many municipal bond issuers attempt to level the playing field between institutions and retail customers during an underwriting. These issuers require underwriters to provide retail order periods. For one or several days, only retail customers may place orders. Then these orders will be filled at the prices paid by institutional customers when the sale is complete. Buying bonds during the underwriting period also does not involve a markup because the issuer pays for it as part of the spread that the underwriters earn.

Virtually all trades, whether institutional or retail, must be reported to the MSRB within 15 minutes of the execution, and there are efforts to lower that time limit. These trades are reported on the MSRB's website.

EMMA

Here we are going to jump into the market through the MSRB's Electronic Municipal Market Access (EMMA) website. This is a public website that provides data about issues and issuers in the municipal market. EMMA is still early in its development, but it already contains a great deal of information. Importantly, EMMA shows all the trades and prices taking place in the market close to when they occur; eventually it will be in near real time. The reporting time keeps shrinking. Now, it is minutes, but it will eventually be seconds.

The scope of the municipal bond market is large. There are more than 80,000 potential issuers and more than a million different securities. By contrast, in corporate equities, there are about 5,700 public companies listed on the major domestic exchanges and about 22,000 different securities.

Historical data on trades are available from January 1, 2005, and some official disclosure documents dating from 1990 can be obtained on EMMA. The site collects information on municipal notes and bonds, and also on 529 college savings plans, which are categorized as municipal securities. A note in the municipal market has a maturity of 13 months or less, although the term is sometimes used generically to describe a short-term bond of two years or shorter. This is to be contrasted with Treasuries, where a Treasury note has a maturity of from two to ten years.

The 529 college savings plans are named after Section 529 of the Internal Revenue Code. These are state-level plans that come with a variety of terms. Generally, they allow a donor to establish a trust for the education of a family member. The money is contributed after tax and so is not a deduction from earnings for tax purposes. The earnings of the 529 trust accumulate tax free, though, so that the student does not owe taxes on the money when it is withdrawn if it is used to pay for college expenses. Each state sets its own rules subject to the federal tax restrictions.

Today the price history of a municipal bond is available on the Internet, but historically, trading of municipal bonds has been opaque to the public. Most municipal bonds are not traded on an organized exchange like the New York Stock Exchange, although organized exchanges have consistently tried to develop active markets in municipal bonds in recent years.

In the early 1900s, both municipal and corporate bonds were actively traded on the New York Stock Exchange. Trading of municipal bonds on the exchange came to a halt at the beginning of 1929. The same process also occurred for corporate bonds, only it happened later, in the middle of the 1940s. Trading of bonds moved from an organized exchange to an over-the-counter (OTC) environment. An OTC market is a decentralized market where trades are normally executed by voice or electronically.

The change occurred as institutions replaced individuals as the marginal buyers for bonds. As a result, the market was restructured as a negotiated market that suited institutional customers.

Exchanges also had other difficulties with institutional customers for bonds. Large, irregular order sizes are a problem for market makers on an exchange. The dollar flows from institutions are larger than those from retail customers and can be highly variable, causing market making in bonds on an exchange to be a risky business. Even without these problems, the institutions that are buying and selling may have an informational advantage over an exchange's market makers, creating a prohibitively costly environment for an exchange.

The OTC environment thus can be more cost-efficient for an institution. Average trading costs have been found to be larger in the OTC market than on an exchange, but this can be very misleading. Transaction costs fall dramatically with transaction size, making the OTC market appealing for institutions, which typically trade in much larger quantities than individuals do.

Many municipal bonds are also traded through electronic platforms where computers match offers and sales. The size of these platforms is growing rapidly. Firms like TMC Bonds LLC offer anonymous order matching of buyers and sellers. In addition, there are numerous proposals for expanded electronic trading.

Whether a trade takes place in the OTC market or on an exchange, it now must be reported to EMMA. In addition, issuers provide the public with information about their bond issues through EMMA. This includes a variety of continuing disclosures.

Trades that are reported to EMMA are identified by time and by the nature of the parties involved in the purchases and sales. There are two types of trading entities. Buyers or sellers who are not dealers or brokers are customers, and trades with them are registered as "customer bought" or "customer sold." It is assumed that the customer bought the bonds from or sold them to a broker/dealer. Trades among brokers and dealers are referred to as "interdealer trades."

The EMMA trading data have been carefully studied to identify the level and pattern of municipal bond trading costs. The cost of trading is the difference between the price dealers will pay, or the bid price, and the price at which they will sell, or the asked price. This bid-asked spread is large for retail-sized trades because the information, transaction, and regulatory costs are large compared to the size of the trade. For most purposes, "retail-sized trades" generally refers to those worth less than $100,000 (100 bonds).

The bid-asked spread falls dramatically as the size of the trade increases. For a trade of about $100,000, the bid-asked spread has been above 1 percent. By the time the trade reaches $10,000,000, the bid-asked spread falls dramatically as a percentage of the value of the trade. The bid-asked spread does not rely significantly on the frequency with which the bond trades. In addition, lower-rated bonds and those with a lot of special features tend to be more expensive to trade.

The liquidity of smaller-sized trades has declined in recent years. In a recent study by the U.S. Government Accountability Office (GAO), the bid-asked spreads between dealers were examined by year, using the EMMA data.

GAO computed a mean spread that was the average of the dealer spreads as a percentage of the average purchase price. The study held other factors constant and found that spreads declined rapidly for every $10,000 increase in the amount of the trade. Table 2-1 shows that in 2010, the mean spread declined by 0.42 percent for every increment of $10,000. It also shows that the effect of increasing size in a trade is more than twice as great in 2010 as it was in 2007. Essentially, the data show that now more than ever, individuals should avoid actively trading small blocks of bonds.

The GAO also looked at the effect of trade size on the dispersion of the trade prices. This analysis asks how the tightness of the prices seen in the market is affected by

Table 2-1   Percentage Change in Spread per $10,000 Increase in Trade Amount

Year	Mean Spread
2005	−0.29%
2006	−0.23%
2007	−0.19%
2008	−0.33%
2009	−0.41%
2010	−0.42%

Source: GAO.

the size of the trade. Table 2-2 shows that the range of prices occurring in the market for both dealer sales to investors and dealer purchases from investors falls rapidly as the size of the trade increases. Interestingly, the price dispersion of sales to customers in 2010 fell more than twice as fast for each $10,000 as in earlier years. The price dispersion data are consistent with a less liquid and less efficient market.

The lesson for retail investors again is that they should not expect to beat the market by rapid trading of small municipal

Table 2-2   Change in Price Dispersion per $10,000 Increase in Trade Amount

Year	Sales	Purchases
2005	−0.14%	−0.04%
2006	−0.11%	−0.03%
2007	−0.13%	−0.04%
2008	−0.41%	−0.26%
2009	−0.39%	−0.19%
2010	−0.33%	−0.15%

Source: GAO.

bond lots. For even the best traders, the trading costs are likely to exceed any capital gains. This helps explain why municipal bond investors tend to buy the bonds and hold them to maturity. In fact, it is arguable that the retail trading that one does see—and most secondary market sales are retail trades—is liquidity-driven and not informational. That is, the bond sales are being forced by the holder's need for cash, not by the availability of new information about the issuer. Individuals who are engaged in forced sales will probably be willing to accept wider bid-asked spreads.

But as many retail trades as there are, these prices are unlikely to be a price-setting mechanism. Rather, the new-issue institutional market is usually the place where the price for a municipal bond is set.

The EMMA data show that the municipal bond market can offer investors exceptional investment opportunities but generally not great trading opportunities. The municipal market has some surprising features. Prices of municipal bonds, for example, tend to rise faster than they fall. Not too surprisingly, this maximizes the broker/dealer's profits.

Examining EMMA Trades

Now, we can examine a few EMMA trades. EMMA reports the trades as it receives them on the Market Activity page, with the most recent at the top. Each line is an individual trade. See Figure 2-1.

First, the date and time of the trade are listed. The trade date for the most recent transaction was at 9:20 a.m. on 5/31/2012. This is the trade date, not the settlement date.

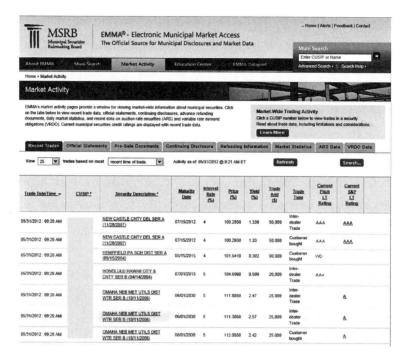

Figure 2-1   EMMA Market Activity Page

The rest of the details of the trade are listed from left to right. Next to the trade date is the unique identifier for the security, the CUSIP. CUSIP is the acronym for Committee on Uniform Securities Identification Procedures. A CUSIP is a nine-digit-and-letter sequence, with the first six identifying the issuer. CUSIPs are ubiquitous in the securities industry and are used for corporate bonds, equities, and many other types of securities domestically and internationally.

The CUSIP is followed by a description of the security. You might think that a security description of "New Castle County Delaware Series A," shown in Figure 2-1 as "NEW CASTLE CNTY DEL SER A (11/28/2007)," would be sufficient, but it is not even close.

Investors who have seen the thousands of bonds listed in the holdings of a large mutual fund or bank will understand that no combination of textual description elements will be sufficient. The only way to be sure exactly which bond one is talking about is to use the CUSIP to identify it, not the security description or the name of the issuer.

Returning to the EMMA example in Figure 2-1, we see that the bond's maturity date of 7/15/2012 is listed next to the description. The maturity of the bond is the date after which the issuer is no longer obliged to pay interest and on which the principal amount, also called the *face value*, is due to be paid to the bondholder. After a bond matures, it is no longer a liability of the issuer.

The *interest rate* is listed next to the maturity date. The term *interest rate* can be confusing. Economically speaking, the interest rate on a bond is the bond's yield, not the "interest rate" listed in EMMA's table. The interest rate used in the table is the coupon rate. This is a percentage of the face value of the bond, and it determines the regular amount of interest that the bondholder receives. Most municipal bonds pay a fixed dollar amount of interest at regular intervals, normally twice a year. The purchaser of the bond will receive this annuity of coupon payments as long as it holds the bond. Any interruption of the timely payment of the coupons is a default.

For every $1,000 in face value, a bond with a 5 percent coupon will pay $50 per year. The convention in the municipal bond market is for payments to be made semiannually, so the investor will get $25 every six months on the coupon payment days. The last payment, at the maturity of the bond, will be $1,025 for every $1,000 of face value, which includes interest for the last six-month period and the return of the principal amount of $1,000.

Understanding Coupons

There are several different types of coupons, including fixed and variable. Coupons can be zero, in which case all the interest on the bond issue is paid to the bondholder at maturity. Variable-rate bonds, as the name implies, allow the interest rate on the bond to change over time. Variable-rate bonds often have long maturities but coupons that are based on short-term rates.

Variable rate demand obligations (VRDOs) are an example of a type of long-term bond with a coupon that changes as short-term rates change. As a result, they are floating-rate bonds. In addition, the VRDO also contains a liquidity feature that allows the holder to put the bond back to a third party. The result is a long-term bond that is effectively a floating-rate short-term instrument. In some cases, the bonds can have more than one coupon mode. These mixed-modal bonds allow the issuer to vary the coupon payment type over the life of the bond and move between fixed and floating coupons. Of course, the existence of the bond's mixed-modal structure is disclosed to the bondholder before the purchase of the bond.

The History of Coupons

The term *coupon* is one of several terms that refer to nineteenth-century techniques for buying and selling securities. In those days, bonds were purchased at banks, and the teller would hand the bonds to the buyer "over the counter."

What the buyer got was a piece of paper with the name of the issuer, the basic agreement, and the face value printed on it.

Attached to this piece of paper were sheets of small squares, called coupons, that instructed the paying agent, normally the local bank, to "pay to the bearer of" the bond a certain dollar amount. The bearer of the bond was the person carrying the bond into the bank. The bonds were thus called *bearer bonds*.

Bearer bonds are generally not issued in the municipal bond market anymore. In fact, tax-exempt bonds cannot be sold as bearer bonds. Instead of bearer bonds being issued, ownership of the bond is recorded electronically in a centralized registry.

In the nineteenth century, the bondholder cut or "clipped" the coupon on the interest payment date, the date printed on the coupon, and delivered it to the bank. The bank paid the bearer the amount that was printed on the coupon. Although this is not today's procedure, we have retained the use of the term *coupon*.

Return to the EMMA Example

Next to the interest rate, EMMA lists the price. This is the percentage of the face value of the bond that the customer pays or receives. If the price of the bond is equal to 100 percent of the face amount, it is said to be a *par bond*. Bonds with prices in excess of 100 percent are referred to as *premium bonds*, and bonds with prices below 100 percent are referred to as *discount bonds*. Designating the bond as a premium bond or a discount bond does not imply anything about the quality of the bond. Rather, for premium bonds, the coupon is simply larger than the yield, and for discount bonds, the coupon is smaller than the yield.

Bonds accrue interest from the issuer over time. The price listed is the *clean price*, which does not include the accrued interest, or the portion of the next coupon that the current bondholder owns when the bond is sold. (Accrued interest is discussed later in this chapter.) When the accrued interest is included in the price, it is referred to as a *dirty* (or *full*) *price*. Bonds that trade without accrued interest are said to trade *flat*. Bonds trading flat are unusual, and often these bonds are in default and not paying coupon interest.

Trade Symbols

W	When Issued
B	Broker's Broker
P	Weighted Average Price
L	List Price

In this example from EMMA, the price percentage at which the trade took place was 100.2930; that is, the purchaser is paying 100.2930 percent of the face value, or $1,002.93 for every thousand dollars of face value. The yield percentage listed next to the price is the interest rate that the buyer expects to earn. The yield calculations involve a variety of assumptions.

As a matter of regulation, the yield listed here is the "yield to worst." Technically, this is the discount rate (internal rate of return) the buyer will get under the worst likely scenario. The yield-to-worst calculation assumes that the bond will not default on any payments, but that if the issuer can exercise any options to lower its cost on the issue, it will do so.

Sometimes the yield is designated with a *W*. When the issuer sells bonds to investors, the trades are said to be in the *primary market*. However, it may be several weeks after the issuance before the actual settlement takes place and the money is given to the issuer. Between the time when the issuer commits to selling the bonds and the settlement date when the money changes hands, the bonds can trade in the market. In that case, the trades are said to be "when issued" and are indicated in EMMA as (W)—a "when-issued trade." The buyer of the bonds on a when-issued trade will get the bonds when the issuer delivers them.

Another special type of trade is a broker's broker trade, designated by a (B). This is an interdealer trade that is facilitated by a third party called the broker.

It sometimes takes a number of trades to fill an order from a customer. When that happens, a single entry may be given for the whole transaction. This is indicated by (P)—a weighted-average-price trade. Another type of trade occurs on the first day of the new issue. This is the list offering price/takedown trade, indicated by (L).

The next column, "Trade Amt ($)," represents the face value of the bonds traded. In many cases, the minimum size of the face value, the minimum denomination, is specified. This minimum is set by the issuer. It is the minimum commercial size for the trades. For very short-term securities, this is frequently $100,000. Longer-term bonds generally have minimum denominations of $5,000 or five bonds, and trades must occur in even multiples of the minimum denomination.

If the trade amount is equal to or more than $1,000,000, the trade is said to be an institutional trade rather than a retail trade on EMMA. At this time, multimillion-dollar trades have the trade price and yield reported with a substantial lag. There are proposals, however, to have these trades reported with the others. Doing so would greatly help to level the information field in trading.

All of the price and yield calculations are the same regardless of what type of customer is buying or selling the bonds. The customer trade type indicates whether it is a customer bought, customer sold, or interdealer trade.

EMMA now lists the current ratings from two rating agencies: Fitch and Standard & Poor's. This bond is rated AAA by both, which is a prime grade.

UNDERSTANDING ACCRUED INTEREST

The purchase and sale of a municipal bond can happen on any business day, not just on coupon payment days. This can happen only because the interest accrues to the holders of the bonds as time passes between coupon payment dates. Coupon interest is paid by the issuer to the registered holder of the bond on the payment date set out in the bond documents. Usually this is at six-month intervals.

If the bond is sold halfway between the coupon payment dates, for example, the coupon will still be paid on its scheduled date, but the seller owns the half of it that has accrued to him while he held the bond. The new buyer needs to pay the seller this accrued interest when she purchases the bond. Thus the seller gets half of the coupon when the bond is sold, and the buyer gets the full coupon on the coupon payment date.

Most municipal bonds accrue interest on a 30/360-day basis, although there are other conventions depending on the type of security. That is, each day represents 1/30 of a month, and each month is 1/12 of a year. The MSRB gives the following formula:

Accrued interest = interest rate × par value × (number of days/360)

Again, the interest rate is the coupon rate on the bond. The number of days is the number of days from the last payment date up to but not including the settlement date. The settlement date is the day when the bonds are delivered and payment for them is made. That payment is the full price, which includes both the price for the bond and the accrued interest.

The MSRB gives an example of calculating accrued interest. Ms. Smith bought $100,000 of municipal bonds in the secondary market. The bonds had a 7 percent coupon rate and paid interest semiannually on December 1 and June 1. Settlement was April 12.

The number of accrued days is 30 times the number of whole months. The last payment date was December 1, which gives 4 whole months, or 120 (4 × 30) accrual days. In April, there are 11 days up to but not including the settlement date of April 12. Thus, there are 131 (120 + 11) accrual days.

Accrued interest = 0.07 × 100,000 × (131/360)
= $2,547.22 to be paid by the buyer to the
seller at settlement

DEALER QUOTATIONS

Dealers list bonds for sale on computer screens and in newspapers. These often include price or yield quotes. Most municipal bonds are quoted on a yield or a yield spread basis. The yield spread is usually the number of basis points (a basis point is 1/100 of a percent) in excess of the yield of a bond with the highest credit quality of the same maturity as the bond being quoted.

The quotes or indications can be "firm" or "subject." Unless a quote is firm, the buyer cannot assume that the seller is committed to a transaction at that price. Prices in the market move quickly, and the vast majority of quotes are subject.

Figure 2-2 shows a slice-in-time offering screen from the Bloomberg PICK system, which is used by institutions

```
1                                                      Muni  PICK
97<GO> to show spreads, 98<GO> to show MSRB trades
The Bloomberg PICK    ALL OFFERINGS                  Page 1 of 2050
 1)   90M PHOENIX ARIZ INDL DEV AUTH ED ARI AZ     6.250 07/01/21       6.250 NET
      NA/NA/NA       SINKING FUND           71885FAM9 STIFEL DEN(303)291-5322
 2)  165M WICHITA KANS SER 806          KS     4.000 12/01/26       3.700 NET
      Aa1/AA+/NA     CA:20@100.000         967244YB4 STIFEL DEN(303)291-5322
 3)  160M WICHITA KANS SER 806          KS     4.000 12/01/25       3.550 NET
      Aa1/AA+/NA     CA:20@100.000         967244YA6 STIFEL DEN(303)291-5322
 4)  245M WICHITA KANS SER 806          KS     4.000 12/01/24       3.400 NET
      Aa1/AA+/NA     CA:20@100.000         967244XZ2 STIFEL DEN(303)291-5322
 5)  135M WICHITA KANS SER 806          KS     3.500 12/01/22       3.050 NET
      Aa1/AA+/NA     CA:20@100.000         967244XX7 STIFEL DEN(303)291-5322
 6)  225M WICHITA KANS SER 806          KS     3.250 12/01/21       2.800 NET
      Aa1/AA+/NA     CA:20@100.000         967244XW9 STIFEL DEN(303)291-5322
 7)  220M WICHITA KANS SER 806          KS     3.000 12/01/20       2.630 NET
      Aa1/AA+/NA     NON-CALLABLE          967244XV1 STIFEL DEN(303)291-5322
 8)   20M WICHITA KANS SER 806          KS     2.750 12/01/19       2.400 NET
      Aa1/AA+/NA     NON-CALLABLE          967244XU3 STIFEL DEN(303)291-5322
 9)   20M WICHITA KANS SER 806          KS     2.000 12/01/16       1.350 NET
      Aa1/AA+/NA     NON-CALLABLE          967244XR0 STIFEL DEN(303)291-5322
10)   65M WICHITA KANS SER 806          KS     2.000 12/01/15       1.050 NET
      Aa1/AA+/NA     NON-CALLABLE          967244XQ2 STIFEL DEN(303)291-5322
11)  185M WICHITA KANS SER 806          KS     2.000 12/01/14       0.770 NET
      Aa1/AA+/NA     NON-CALLABLE          967244XP4 STIFEL DEN(303)291-5322
Australia 61 2 9777 8600 Brazil 5511 3048 4500 Europe 44 20 7330 7500 Germany 49 69 9204 1210 Hong Kong 852 2977 6000
Japan 81 3 3201 8900     Singapore 65 6212 1000     U.S. 1 212 318 2000     Copyright 2011 Bloomberg Finance L.P.
                                            SN 602456 EDT  GMT-4:00 G989-1173-0 15-Jul-2011 11:19:50
```

Figure 2-2 Bloomberg PICK Screen (*Source:* Bloomberg L.P. Used with permission of Bloomberg L.P. Copyright © 2012. All rights reserved.)

to locate buyers and sellers for specific bonds. These bonds are then typically resold to individual investors.

The first offering is for $90,000 (90M) in face value of the Phoenix, Arizona, Industrial Development Authority. It has a coupon of 6.25 percent and matures on 07/01/2021. The bond is not rated by any of the top three rating agencies (NA/NA/NA) and has a sinking fund requiring the issuer to deposit funds in a trust for the early retirement of the bond. It is offered at a yield of 6.25 percent. The offer is subject, so it may be changed at any time, and the potential buyer can call the Denver office of the firm (DEN) at the number listed to negotiate the trade.

Figure 2-3 shows a page from the Bloomberg bid wanted system. This page gives a list of institutional investors (the

<HELP> for explanation, <MENU> for similar functions.   Muni **MBWD**

91) View All	92) Msg Alert		Page 1/2 Municipal Bids Wanted - Sellside Firm Menu		
Firm Name		Items		Firm Name	Items
1) ATLANTIC TRUST GROUP INC		1	22)	FRANKLIN MUNICIPALS	2
2) B.T. PRIVATE BANK		11	23)	GANNETT WELSH & KOTLER INC	28
3) BEL AIR INV		1	24)	GOLDMAN ASSET MANAGEMENT	50
4) BESSEMER TRUST		14	25)	HARRIS TRUST & SAVINGS BK	2
5) BLACKROCK SMA		20	26)	HUNTINGTON NAT'L BANK	20
6) BOSTON COMPANY		139	27)	INTERCONTINENTAL	6
7) BRECKINRIDGE CAP ADV		110	28)	JP MORGAN FLEMING ASSET	59
8) BROWN INVESTMENT ADVISORY		13	29)	JP MORGAN INVESTMENT ADV	17
9) C W HENDERSON		8	30)	LAZARD ASSET MANAGEMENT	4
10) CAP RESEARCH		6	31)	LORD ABBETT & COMPANY	4
11) CITY NATL INVEST/ADVISORS		3	32)	LYDIAN BANK & TRUST	9
12) COLUMBIA MGMT ADVISORS		2	33)	M&I INVESTMENTS	7
13) CONNING ASSET MANAGEMENT		7	34)	MERRILL TEST CUSTOMER	2
14) DEUTSCHE BANK		1	35)	MORGAN STANLEY MGD. ACCTS.	12
15) DeAM-BOSTON		5	36)	NEUBERGER-BERMAN	69
16) EAGLE ASSET MANAGEMENT		46	37)	NORTHERN TRUST BK-CHICAGO	26
17) EATON VANCE MUNICIPALS		12	38)	NORTHERN TRUST-SHORT TERM	1
18) EATON VANCE TABS		35	39)	NORWEST BANK, MINNESOTA	36
19) FEDERATED RESEARCH CORP.		8	40)	NUVEEN ADVISORY CHICAGO	3
20) FIFTH THIRD ASSET MGT		23	41)	NUVEEN SMA	17
21) FIRST INVESTORS MGMT.		1	42)	PAYDEN & RYGEL INV COUNSEL	1

Australie 61 2 9777 8600 Brazil 5511 3048 4500 Europe 44 20 7330 7500 Germany 49 69 9204 1210 Hong Kong 852 2977 6000
Japan 81 3 3201 8900   Singapore 65 6212 1000   U.S. 1 212 318 2000   Copyright 2011 Bloomberg Finance L.P.
SN 682456 EDT GMT-4:00 6989-1173-0 15-Jul-2011 11:20:19

Figure 2-3   Investors Requesting Bids on Their Bonds

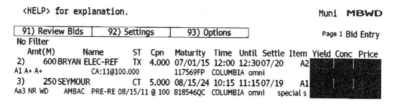

Figure 2-4   Municipal Bond Bid Wanted Screen (*Source:* Bloomberg L.P. Used with permission of Bloomberg L.P. Copyright © 2012. All rights reserved.)

"buy side"). They range from familiar mutual funds to a variety of banks. The first one listed, Atlantic Trust Group Inc., has one bond on which it is seeking a buyer to make a bid.

Figure 2-4 shows two bonds offered by different firms. In the first bond listed, the firm is asking the buyer to enter a firm bid by 12:00 that is good until 12:30. The bid can be either a yield or a price. A small reduction in the market price is sometimes also provided as a transaction cost. This is the concession (Conc). Bonds trade for dollar amounts, but it is generally more convenient to convert those prices to a type of economic interest rate, the yield. One price can be converted to any number of yields using a wide variety of equations with different assumptions. In Figure 2-4, we see that the yields given are the lower of the yield calculated to the optional call date or to maturity, given a price. This is the yield to worst, and regulations require that it be shown to the customer.

3

Reading an Official Statement

A municipal bond is a loan to a state or local government. The detailed terms of the loan are contained in a lengthy contract between the issuer and bondholders called an *indenture*. It defines the rights and responsibilities of the issuer and the bondholders including the detailed covenants of the loan. Regulations require that the most relevant details of the trade be disclosed to buyers upon or before the completion of the trade. Generally, the trade is completed when the money changes hands on the settlement date. Many of these relevant details are contained in the indenture.

In the corporate market, issuers are required to assemble and distribute a prospectus for each issue. The prospectus is subject to strict requirements established by the Securities and Exchange Commission (SEC). State and local issuers are not subject to such rigorous rules, but issuers do produce, or have produced for them, a disclosure document called the *official statement* (OS). An official statement is a slice-in-time picture showing the essential elements of the agreement and the status of the issuer.

Each OS is different. Today, the OS is disseminated through EMMA, but EMMA's holdings are far from complete. Investors are strongly encouraged to get an OS from their broker or the seller and read it before investing in a municipal bond. This chapter provides a general view of what an OS should be expected to contain. The point of this presentation is not to cover every detail. Rather, it is to serve as a guide to what to look for and where one might find it. The investor is not expected to be a credit expert. That having been said, the OS can give a broad indication of whether the bond is likely to be a suitable investment and what questions might be relevant to pursue.

In this chapter, we will also look at some of the more important features of a bond issue by examining one in some detail. This will give us an introduction to a number of topics that will be revisited in more detail later.

THE PRELIMINARY OFFICIAL STATEMENT

Before the sale of a new bond, a preliminary official statement (POS) is usually produced. At that time, the sale has not yet taken place, so the exact details of the bonds and the prices at which they will be offered are not known. The POS is often referred to as a "red herring," as the title "PRELIMINARY OFFICIAL STATEMENT" and declarations that the data are preliminary are written in red around the edges of the front cover. See Figure 3-1.

PRELIMINARY OFFICIAL STATEMENT
STATE OF ILLINOIS

Figure 3-1   Preliminary Official Statement

This POS was produced on March 31, 2009, and should be considered accurate on that date. Investors need to be conscious of the fact that the OS and POS are not revised through time. Updating the information about the issuer and the bonds is done through the continuing disclosure provisions in EMMA, and, unfortunately, the issuers often fail to provide the agreed-upon updates. When there is no continuing disclosure, it is definitely caveat emptor for the investor.

The first sale of a bond occurs in the primary market, and this sale of a State of Illinois bond is an example of such a sale. The bonds can be sold directly to the final buyer in a private placement. Usually, however, the bonds are underwritten. In an underwriting, the entire bond issue is sold to one or a syndicate of financial intermediaries, who in turn sell the bonds to buyers in smaller pieces. Formally this is known as denomination intermediation.

Special Bond Terms

The bond market uses a specialized vocabulary. Most terms are available in SIFMA's Glossary of Bond Terms at http://investinginbonds.com. A Glossary of Acronyms can be found at the back of this book.

In normally functioning markets, the entire issue is sold to the underwriters in an "all-or-none" (AON) sale. If there is not enough demand for the issue at what the issuer considers to be a reasonable price, the sale may be withdrawn. However, this is unusual. Issues are rarely withdrawn, since the issuer will normally premarket the bonds and not bring them to market when there is any doubt about their getting a good reception.

Failed underwritings can occur during market disruptions, and in these market conditions, the issuer may sell the bonds on a best-efforts basis. This allows the underwriters to buy as many bonds from the issuer as they can sell, even if this is less than the entire issue. Very few issues are best efforts. The amount sold must ordinarily be sufficient to finance a project.

As we can see in Figure 3-2, the State of Illinois offered $150,000,000 in par value for sale on April 7, 2009. The bonds were sold through competitive bids, and bids had to be received before 11:00 a.m. on that date. In the past, the bids were hand-delivered, but for most sales, those days have long passed. Today, electronic bidding systems are used.

The bonds are payable from the general taxing power of the state, and so are *general obligation bonds* or GO bonds. State law is quite specific about how these bonds may be sold. The POS states, "GO Bonds issued within a fiscal year must be sold pursuant to notice of sale and public bid."

$150,000,000
GENERAL OBLIGATION BONDS,
SERIES OF APRIL, 2009
DATE OF SALE: APRIL 7, 2009
Bids Will Be Received Until 11:00 A. M. Central Daylight Savings Time
Preliminary Official Statement Printed   March 31, 2009
Expected Date of Issuance (Delivery): April 14, 2009

Figure 3-2   Time of Sale

The state must publish an official notice of sale. *The Bond Buyer* newspaper is a common place for such a publication. The notice will tell potential bidders where to find the requirements for the bid, such as what maturities and interest rates are allowed, as well as how to make the bid. A good-faith deposit may be required.

The bonds are sold to the underwriter that offers the issuer the highest dollar price or lowest interest rate. The issuer will specify how the interest rate is to be calculated. Most issues now specify that the true interest cost (TIC) be used. This is the interest rate that causes the discounted cash flows of all the bonds in the issue to equal the price paid for the bonds.

Determining the TIC is a complicated calculation, and in the days before computers were widely available, a simpler interest-rate calculation, the net interest cost (NIC), was used. The NIC does not employ proper discounting of the cash flows, and so when it is used, there must be a set of strict constraints to ensure that the bonds awarded through an NIC bid go to the bidder offering the highest dollar price.

Before the sale, the underwriters can take indications of interest from potential buyers, but they cannot take orders to buy. The OS makes this clear, as shown in Figure 3-3.

No dealer, broker, salesperson, or other person has been authorized by the State of Illinois or the Purchasers to give any information or to make any representations other than those contained in this Official Statement.... This Official Statement does not constitute an offer to sell or the solicitation of an offer to buy, nor shall there be any sale of the Bonds by any person in any jurisdiction in which it is unlawful for such person to make such offer, solicitation or sale.

Figure 3-3 Not an Offer

Nor can a dealer or broker "mark up" or comment on the POS to point out features of the bonds that it might think would be important to a buyer.

The alternative to a competitive sale is a negotiated sale. In a negotiated sale, the issuer normally interviews several competing underwriters to see which one is most likely to minimize the interest cost to the issuer. There have been a myriad of studies of negotiated versus competitive sales in municipal bonds. The general sense is that competitive sales offer greater efficiency, if only because there is less chance of anticompetitive influences. As a practical matter, for frequent issuers, the best choice in well-functioning markets is probably to issue the bonds competitively. For infrequent, lower-quality issuers or issues with complex structures, the cost of developing the internal talent to handle an issue is not likely to be justified, and a negotiated sale is probably the best. Most issues are negotiated, however, and as the complexity of the regulations governing municipal issuance grows, ever more outsourcing to experts can be expected.

THE SOURCE OF PAYMENTS

How will the bonds be repaid? The source of the funds to be used for payments on the bonds is spelled out in the POS in the security section, a portion of which is shown in Figure 3-4.

Here we see that these bonds are direct, general obligations of the state and that the pledge of the "full faith and credit of the State" is "irrepealable," meaning that the state legislature cannot pass a law repealing the state's duty to pay

SECURITY
DIRECT, GENERAL OBLIGATIONS

The Bonds, together with all other GO Bonds, are direct, general obligations of the State, and by law the full faith and credit of the State is pledged for the punctual payment of interest on the Bonds as the interest becomes due and for the punctual payment of the principal thereof at maturity, or any earlier redemption date, and premium, if any. The Bond Act provides that the sections of the Bond Act making such pledge are irrepealable until all GO Bonds issued under the Bond Act, including the Bonds, have been paid in full.

Figure 3-4   Security Summary

off the bonds. The process of repayment is also spelled out in the provision shown in Figure 3-5.

The General Assembly is thus required by law to pay the bondholders on time. As a result, GOs as a class have been the most secure type of municipal bond. No bond, however, is completely risk-free, and the investor should follow the financial status of the issuer in EMMA.

Not all municipal bonds are GOs. Many municipal bonds are *revenue bonds*, where the funds for the payment of interest and repayment of principal come only from a specific revenue source, not the general taxing power of the issuer. Many revenue bonds, such as water and sewer bonds, are nevertheless very secure investments. Bonds that are payable

STATE FUNDING PAYMENTS

To provide for the manner of repayment of the Bonds, the Bond Act requires the Governor to include an appropriation in each annual State Budget. . . . The Bond Act also creates a separate fund. . . . The Bond Act requires the General Assembly to annually make appropriations to pay the principal of, interest on and premium, if any, on outstanding Bonds.

Figure 3-5   Annual Appropriations

from both tax revenues and specific project revenues are said to be "double barreled."

GOs need to be distinguished from "moral obligation bonds." The POS indicates that some issuers in the state issue moral obligation bonds, as shown in Figure 3-6. These are not obligations of the state, but the local issuer or authority that is selling moral obligation bonds can appeal to the state for help in repaying the bonds if it needs to. The state is not required by statute to help the issuer, but the legislature has the moral obligation to help. Even though the bond issue is a GO, full disclosure requires that the issuer include information about all the debt that it may be liable to repay under any condition.

Moral obligation bonds can be very secure bonds, but the first analysis is the credit of the issuer, not the backing of the state.

MORAL OBLIGATION BONDS

Currently, eight entities in the State may issue moral obligation bonds. The moral obligation pledge generally provides that in the event the authority issuing moral obligation bonds determines that revenue available to the authority will be insufficient for the payment of principal and interest on such bonds during the next State fiscal period, the authority shall certify to the Governor the amount required to pay such principal and interest and any amounts withdrawn from bond reserve funds to pay principal and interest on moral obligation bonds. The Governor shall then submit the amounts so certified to the General Assembly. The Governor's recommendations for these and all other State appropriations are a matter of executive discretion. Thus, the moral obligation pledge does not constitute a legally enforceable obligation of the Governor to recommend a State appropriation. Moreover, the General Assembly is not statutorily required to make an appropriation for the amount so certified by the authority, nor must the Governor sign any such appropriation bill if passed by the General Assembly.

Debt evidenced by moral obligation bonds is not debt of the State, and is not secured by any State funds.

Figure 3-6   Moral Obligations, Not GOs

THE FINAL OFFICIAL STATEMENT

After the sale of the bond, the final official statement, the OS, must be issued. Official statements are not continuously updated, although issuers frequently give supplementary financial information. The SEC does not require state and local governments to provide quarterly or annual information the way a corporation does, although many agree to do so voluntarily. The lack of ongoing disclosure is a continuing problem in the municipal bond market, and bonds that lack it should be carefully scrutinized. These bonds may be highly illiquid, trading at prices well below those of other comparable bonds.

The OS contains the results of the sale. These are shown in Figure 3-7.

The shorter-maturity bonds are called *serial bonds*. In this case, the bonds maturing in each year from 2010 through 2029 have $6 million in face value and are the serials in the issue. Each of these bonds has its own price and yield. For example, the bonds maturing in 2020 have a coupon of 4.75 percent and at the time of issuance were sold to yield 4.130 percent. Because the coupon is larger than the yield, this is a premium bond. And because it traded at a premium when it was newly issued, it is called an *original issue premium*, or OIP.

After issuance, the yields on this bond may rise or fall, causing the bond to trade at prices below or above the original issue price. Original issue premium bonds, however, retain the designation as OIP even when they trade in the secondary market, since the amount of the original issue premium affects their tax treatment.

The purpose of this Official Statement Addendum is to set forth the details of sale of the $150,000,000 General Obligation Bonds, Series of April 2009 (*the "Bonds"*), sold by the State of Illinois (the *"State"*) on April 7, 2009. The Bonds will mature on April 1 of each of the years, in the amounts and bearing interest as follows:

Year	Amount	Rate	Yield	Year	Amount	Rate	Yield
2010	$6,000,000	3.00%	1.50%	2021	$6,000,000	5.00%	4.28%
2011	6,000,000	3.00%	1.70%	2022	6,000,000	5.00%	4.43%
2012	6,000,000	3.00%	1.96%	2023	6,000,000	5.00%	4.58%
2013	6,000,000	3.00%	2.39%	2024	6,000,000	5.00%	4.73%
2014	6,000,000	3.00%	2.78%	2025	6,000,000	5.00%	4.87%
2015	6,000,000	4.00%	3.02%	2026	6,000,000	5.00%	4.98%
2016	6,000,000	4.00%	3.26%	2027	6,000,000	5.25%	5.08%
2017	6,000,000	4.00%	3.49%	2028	6,000,000	5.25%	5.17%
2018	6,000,000	4.00%	3.72%	2029	6,000,000	5.25%	5.25%
2019	6,000,000	4.00%	3.94%				
2020	6,000,000	4.75%	4.13%				

$30,000,000 5.25% Term Bonds Due April 1, 2034, Yield 5.396%, Price 98.008

The scheduled payment of principal of and interest on the Bonds maturing on April 1, 2034, which are subject to mandatory redemption by lot on April 1 of the years 2030 through 2034, inclusive, in the amounts set forth below under the caption MANDATORY REDEMPTION OF TERM BONDS.

Figure 3-7   Results

The final bond, with $30,000,000 in face value and a 5.25 percent coupon, matures (is due) on April 1, 2034, when the last principal payment must be made. This bond was sold for a yield of 5.396 percent, and so the bond is a discount bond priced at 98.008. This is an *original issue discount* (OID), and as with an OIP, the bond may trade at par, at a premium, or at a discount in the secondary market over time as interest rates in the market rise and fall. Nevertheless, it will retain its designation as an OID for tax purposes.

Optional Calls

In the redemption provisions of the OS for the bond, shown in Figure 3-8, we see that the state has reserved the choice

REDEMPTION

OPTIONAL REDEMPTION

The Bonds maturing on or after April 1, 2019 are subject to redemption prior to maturity at the option of the State as a whole, or in part, in integral multiples of $5,000, from such maturities as may be selected by the State (less than all of the Bonds of a single maturity to be selected by lot by the Bond Registrar as described under "Redemption Procedure" below), on April 1, 2018, and on any date thereafter, at the redemption price of par plus accrued interest to the redemption date

Figure 3-8   Optional Calls

of retiring some of the bonds prior to their stated maturities. In the first part of the redemption provision, the state has retained the "option" to redeem the bonds maturing on or after April 1, 2019. This means that the state has the right but not the obligation to call the bonds away from the bondholders on or after 2019.

From issuance to the first call date, the bonds cannot be called; they are *call protected*. After that, if interest rates fall enough to justify exercising the call, the issuer is required to pay the bondholders the par value of the bonds, plus any accrued interest. The call would normally be exercised by selling a refunding bond and using the money from that sale to pay the holders of the old bonds. The new issue is called the *refunding issue*, and the old issue is called the *refunded issue*. If only part of the outstanding bonds is called, it is a *partial refunding*.

The exercise of the call is normally the result of interest rates in the market falling after the sale of the bond. This can occur because interest rates in the whole economy have declined or because the rates in the municipal bond sector have fallen relative to other types of rates such as those for Treasury bonds. Bond-specific factors can also lead to a refunding.

Short-term interest rates in the municipal bond market are normally much lower than longer-term rates. We can see that the yield on the 25-year-maturity bond was 5.25 percent. Fifteen years after the sale, these bonds will be 10-year-maturity bonds. They will "roll down" the curve. If nothing has happened in the market, the yield on the bond will now be that of a 10-year-maturity bond, 3.94 percent, and the issuer may want to retire the bonds with a 5.25 percent coupon and replace them with others that yield 3.94 percent.

In addition, an issuer may have been a weak credit when it initially came to market and have had to pay a yield penalty because of its credit condition. Over time, this credit spread may fall, and the issuer may be able to call and retire the old higher-coupon bonds and replace them with new bonds that have a lower (narrower) spread. Other reasons, like changing the indenture to eliminate restrictive covenants or extending the maturity profile of the issuer, can also motivate the use of the call.

Mandatory Calls

In addition to the optional call, the term bonds also have their own special redemption provisions—the mandatory call.

Unlike the optional call provision, the mandatory call spelled out in the redemption provision provides that the state must call and retire part of the issue as provided in the table (see Figure 3-9). Because part of the issue must be retired early and the bonds are picked at random, the effective maturity of the bond is less than 2034. The section at

MANDATORY REDEMPTION OF TERM BONDS

The Term Bonds maturing on April 1, 2034, are subject to mandatory redemption by lot on April 1 of the year and in the amount set forth below at a redemption price equal to the par amount of the Bonds so redeemed plus accrued interest to the redemption date.

YEAR OF MANDATORY REDEMPTION	PRINCIPAL AMOUNT TO BE REDEEMED
2030	$6,000,000
2031	6,000,000
2032	6,000,000
2033	6,000,000
2034 (maturity)	6,000,000

Figure 3-9   Mandatory Calls

the end of this chapter called "Calculation of the Term Bond Average Life" shows a sample calculation of the average life of the bond, which is the expected life of any individual $5,000 bond in the $30,000,000 bond with these mandatory calls.

It is important to note that this is a mandatory redemption. As a result, it doesn't matter what interest rates are on the mandatory redemption date. The issuer is obliged to retire the bonds according to the mandatory redemption schedule at the price specified in the OS.

THE LEGAL OPINION

The official statement also includes the legal opinion (LO), and investors should certainly read this section carefully. In order to prevent fraud and to minimize mistakes in the issuance of municipal bonds (and this is not to be taken lightly), a legal opinion should always be expected to be found in the OS. It contains a valid opinion of an authorized bond counsel. The lawyer acts on behalf of the issuer but, technically, for the benefit of the bondholders, and certifies that the issuer has the authority under state and federal law to sell the bonds. It also states that the procedure under which the bond was issued followed the law. The bond counsel is not independently verifying the data in the official statement, nor is the bond counsel giving an opinion on the appropriateness of a particular bond for investors.

Instead, investors should expect to see that the bond counsel has found that the bonds are as represented. In this case, the state of Illinois has pledged its full faith and credit to repay the bonds, and the bond counsel will need to be sure that the state can do so.

The bond counsel will also check to see that the tax status of the bonds is what the official statement says it is (see Figure 3-10). In this case, the bond counsel found that "interest on the bonds is excludable from gross income for federal income tax purposes." That is, the bonds are tax-exempt at the federal tax level. Notice that this says that the *interest* on the bonds is excludable from gross income.

In the opinion of Bond Counsel, under existing laws, interest on the Bonds is excludable from gross income for federal income tax purposes. . . .

Although Bond Counsel will render an opinion that interest on the Bonds is excludable from gross income for federal income tax purposes, the accrual or receipt of interest on the Bonds may otherwise affect an owner's federal or state tax liability. . . . Prospective purchasers of the Bonds should consult their own tax advisors with regard to the other tax consequences of owning the Bonds.

Under existing laws, interest on the Bonds is not exempt from income taxes imposed by the State of Illinois.

Figure 3-10   Legal Opinion

The holders do not need to include the interest they receive on the bonds in their federal taxable income. This does not mean that the tax-exempt income does not need to be reported to the IRS. Even though it is not taxed, the interest must be reported every year. Nor does the legal opinion say that capital gains and other types of taxes such as estate taxes do not apply. They do.

Most states exempt the interest on bonds sold by entities within the state from state tax, but many do not allow an exemption for out-of-state issues. Here, the state of Illinois has elected to impose state income tax on the interest on its bonds. Interest on the bond "is not exempt from income taxes" imposed by the state.

BOND INSURANCE

The last paragraph on the cover page notes that the term bond's principal and interest are guaranteed by a private insurer, Assured Guaranty Corporation. If the issuer is unable to make payments on this bond, Assured Guaranty Corporation has agreed to stand in its place and make them for the issuer. Further information on this insurer is contained later in another section of the official statement. Most new issues are not insured anymore.

CALCULATION OF THE TERM BOND AVERAGE LIFE

In the OS, the stated maturity value of the 2034 bonds was $30 million. The mandatory redemption schedule will cause part of that $30 million to be paid early. For example, in

Table 3-1   Calculation of Average Life

Year of Redemption	Years from 2009	Amount Redeemed	Percent of Total
2030	21	$6 million	20%
2031	22	$6 million	20%
2032	23	$6 million	20%
2033	24	$6 million	20%
2034	25	$6 million	20%

Source: Author's calculations.

2030, $6 million of the $30 million will be paid. Thus, 20 percent ($6,000,000/$30,000,000) of the 2034 bond is really a 2030 bond. It is often useful to think about the average life of such a bond. Table 3-1 shows the average life calculation for this bond. For simplicity, we will do the arithmetic in whole years.

Each year from 2030 through 2033, 20 percent of the bond issue is to be retired, so that when the final maturity comes in 2034, only the last 20 percent of the issue remains to be paid. As a result, the 2034 bond has an effective maturity, or average life, of 2032, or 23 years.

The average life of the bond can be obtained by multiplying the percent of the total times the years from 2009. Computationally, $23 = (20 \text{ percent} \times 21) + (20 \text{ percent} \times 22) + (20 \text{ percent} \times 23) + (20 \text{ percent} \times 24) + (20 \text{ percent} \times 25)$.

The early retirement of part of the term bond reduces the risk to the bondholders because it avoids a crisis at maturity, when the issuer would have to hold in cash or borrow the full $30 million. A special fund, the sinking fund, is created when the bond is sold to slowly accumulate the amounts necessary for the mandatory retirement of the term bond.

4

A Revenue Bond Example

The Internal Revenue Code specifies who can issue a tax-exempt bond and for what purposes. In general, municipal bonds can be sold by a state or state entity only for public purposes, whether they are taxable or tax-exempt. However, the code is much more specific than this general rule implies when the bond is federally tax-exempt.

Issuers of tax-exempt bonds need to file information reports with the United States. In addition, tax-exempt bonds must be registered and cannot be bearer bonds. Bonds that are directly guaranteed by the federal government cannot be sold on a tax-exempt basis, and there are a bevy of other restrictions as well.

States, political subdivisions of states, and territories like Puerto Rico can sell tax-exempt bonds. In general, the bonds must be governmental. Not only must the purpose be one of providing goods for the public as a whole, but the public must own whatever is acquired with the borrowed money as well.

And here the term *bond* includes long-term bonds, notes, leases, and other debt obligations. *Private-activity bonds* are bonds where a substantial portion of the proceeds (usually more than 10 percent) goes to private entities like corporations. Private-activity bonds are normally taxable. They are allowed to be sold on a tax-exempt basis only if they are "qualified." A private-activity bond is qualified if it's on the list specified by Congress in the tax code as being qualified.

When Congress set up the rules for what private-activity bonds qualified as tax-exempt, it merely made a list. Private-activity bonds that are qualified to be sold as tax-exempt bonds include those for airports, docks, wharves, mass commuting facilities, water, sewage, electricity, and gas. The list goes on to include mortgage bonds, student loan bonds, redevelopment bonds, and bonds for charitable facilities like hospitals.

The list is fairly long, but not all types of bonds are included. Pension bonds, for example, are not included. The list is not an example of the types of bonds that are qualified. A bond of a particular type either is on the list or is taxable.

The overall volume of private-activity bonds issued in a state each year is limited by a state volume cap. The state volume caps for private-activity bonds are a function of population and vary by year. In 2012, state and local governments can sell $32.821 billion of private-activity bonds nationally. Alabama has a private-activity volume cap of $284.56 million, while California has a volume cap of $3.58 billion.

Except for those issued to support some charities, private-purpose municipal bonds are alternative minimum tax (AMT) bonds. The interest on the bond is a "preference item" and is included in the AMT calculation. As a result, these bonds may be taxable to investors paying the AMT.

The states and local governments have created a variety of conduit issuers. These entities issue tax-exempt bonds "on behalf of" private entities like private hospitals. This is possible because for tax purposes, the property financed by the sale of the tax-exempt bonds is treated as though it is owned by a governmental unit. Of course, this is only for tax purposes and does not affect the actual rights to the property. That stays with the private party using the facility.

Here we will examine the basic structure of a revenue bond financing. The bond is a power revenue bond. This is a fairly straightforward revenue bond, and to simplify the discussion even more, it is a refunding bond, so we will not be dealing with the details of a particular construction project. The bond proceeds of a refunding are used to call and retire another loan.

Generally, the entire bond issue does not have to be used for the refunding. A bond issue can and often does have a refunding part and a new money portion. So, for example, an issuer can borrow $200,000,000 and use half of it to call and retire an old bond and half to build a building.

POWER BOND EXAMPLE

The title of the issue appears on the front page of the OS and is shown in Figure 4-1.

$123,120,000

Department of Water and Power of the City of Los Angeles

Power System Revenue Bonds, 2009 Series A

Figure 4-1   Title of Bond Issue

This bond was sold by the Los Angeles Department of Water and Power (LADWP) and had a total face value of $123,120,000. This issuer has many bond issues outstanding and designates this series of serial and term bonds as 2009 Series A. The title immediately identifies the bond as a revenue bond, and therefore it is not going to be repaid from state or local taxes.

The interest and principal payments and any mandatory sinking fund payments make up the debt service on the bond. The issuer could hardly make the revenue bond nature of these payments clearer. Figure 4-2 comes from the middle of the cover.

The ratings on the issue are given on the cover of the OS as Fitch: "AA–," Moody's: "Aa3," and Standard & Poor's: "AA–." So, at the time of issuance, this was a high-quality (investment-grade) issue, but these ratings may change over time. Changes to the rating are a material event and should be disclosed on EMMA. The nature of municipal bond

The Series A Bonds will be special obligations of the Department payable only from the Power Revenue Fund and not out of any other fund or moneys of the Department or the City of Los Angeles (the "City"). The Series A Bonds will not constitute or evidence an indebtedness of the City or a lien or charge on any property or the general revenues of the City. Neither the faith and credit nor the taxing power of the City will be pledged to the payment of the Series A Bonds.

Figure 4-2   Bonds Are Special Obligations

ratings and the controversies surrounding them are explored in the last section of this chapter.

At the top of the cover page in the OS we also have a summary of the tax status of the bonds, as shown in Figure 4-3.

This is less complex than it appears. The legal opinion is given by the bond counsel. Every OS will, or should, have a legal opinion. It would be very unwise for an investor to buy a bond that lacks one. Let's look at one phrase: "interest" on the bonds is "excluded . . . under Section 103." This means that the coupon income and original issue discount are federally tax-exempt because Section 103 on the bonds refers to a section of the federal tax code. The opinion also declares that the interest "is exempt from State of California personal income taxes."

This interest is not a preference item for the AMT. If it were a preference item, the interest would be taxable under the AMT. There are both federal individual and federal corporate AMTs. They are structured differently, but essentially both the individual and the corporation

In the opinion of Orrick, Herrington & Sutcliffe LLP, Bond Counsel to the Department, based on an analysis of existing laws, regulations, rulings and court decisions, and assuming, among other matters, the accuracy of certain representations and compliance with certain covenants, interest on the Series A Bonds (as defined below) is excluded from gross income for federal income tax purposes under Section 103 of the Internal Revenue Code of 1986 and is exempt from State of California personal income taxes. In the further opinion of Bond Counsel, interest on the Series A Bonds is not a specific preference item for purposes of the federal individual or corporate alternative minimum taxes, although Bond Counsel observes that such interest is included in adjusted current earnings when calculating corporate alternative minimum taxable income. Bond Counsel expresses no opinion regarding any other tax consequences related to the ownership or disposition of, or the accrual or receipt of interest on, the Series A Bonds. See "TAX MATTERS" herein.

Figure 4-3   Tax Features

compute their regular tax and their AMT and pay the higher of the two. The top individual AMT rate is 28 percent, and that for corporations is 20 percent. Some municipal bonds have all of their interest included in the AMT. These are generally private-purpose bonds and are designated AMT bonds.

Corporate AMT is especially complex. One item included in the corporate alternative taxable income is the adjusted current earnings (ACE) adjustment. If a bond is an AMT bond, then all the interest is subject to taxation at 20 percent if the corporation pays AMT. Even if the bond is not an AMT bond, a portion of the interest is subject to the AMT through the ACE provision. For a corporation, though, the AMT is not as draconian as it seems because the extra tax that a corporation may pay under the AMT can be used as a credit against future taxes. More details about the taxation of the bond can be found in the tax matters section of the OS.

The debt service on the bonds will be paid out of the Power Revenue Fund, and the power system will receive fees from users. As Figure 4-4 shows, LADWP pledges to set rates that are sufficient to meet the debt service on the bonds.

Since this is a final OS, the underwriting syndicate is given at the bottom of the page with the lead underwriter at the top. See Figure 4-5.

The details of the individual bonds are contained in the maturity schedule, which is typically on page 2 of the OS, although there are many variations. A portion of the schedule from the OS is reproduced in Figure 4-6. The issue has serial bonds maturing from 2010 to 2030.

Rate Covenant

The Department covenants . . . that the Board will fix rates, subject to the approval of the City Council of the City (the "City Council"), for service from the Power System, and collect charges for such service, so as to provide revenues which [are] . . . at least sufficient to pay, as the same shall become due, the principal of and interest on the Outstanding Bonds, and all other outstanding bonds, notes and other evidences of indebtedness payable out of the Power Revenue Fund. . . . During the time the Series A Bonds remain Outstanding, the City Council is required by the Charter to approve electric rates in an amount sufficient to meet all such revenue requirements.

Figure 4-4   Repayment Agreement

De La Rosa & Co.

Citi   *Goldman, Sachs & Co.*   *J.P. Morgan*

Morgan Stanley & Co. Incorporated   *Siebert Brandford Shank & Co., LLC*

Fidelity Capital Market Services   *Ramirez & Co., Inc.*

Figure 4-5   Underwriters

Year	Amount	Rate	Yield	Price	CUSIP No.
2021	2,230,000	5.00	3.80	109.792[c]	
2022	700,000	4.00	3.99	100.077[c]	
2022	2,690,000	5.00	3.99	108.166[c]	
2023	1,025,000	4.13	4.19	99.299	
2023	2,535,000	5.00	4.19	106.486[c]	
2024	1,285,000	4.25	4.36	98.772	
2024	2,450,000	5.00	4.36	105.082[c]	
2025	3,935,000	5.00	4.49	104.024[c]	
2026	245,000	4.50	4.60	98.807	
2026	3,895,000	5.00	4.60	103.138[c]	
2027	4,355,000	5.00	4.71	102.261[c]	
2028	4,585,000	5.00	4.81	101.472[c]	
2029	4,830,000	5.00	4.88	100.924[c]	
2030	5,080,000	5.00	4.94	100.458[c]	

Figure 4-6   Maturity Schedule

*$10,980,000 5.000% Term Bonds due July 1, 2032—Yield 5.040% Price 99.448
CUSIP† No.*   *$12,165,000 5.000% Term Bonds due July 1, 2034—
Yield 5.070% Price 99.000 CUSIP† No.*   *$36,490,000 5.000% Term
Bonds due July 1, 2039—Yield 5.100% Price 98.457 CUSIP† No.*

Figure 4-7   The Term Bonds

There are three term bonds maturing in 2032, 2034, and 2039. Information on these is shown in Figure 4-7.

If we look at the bonds maturing in 2026, we find an interesting structure. There are two separate bonds with the same maturity date, July 1, 2026, but different coupons (see Figure 4-8). These are called *companion bonds*.

One issue has a 4.50 percent coupon at a yield of 4.60 percent. Since the coupon is less than the yield, this is a discount bond. It has a price of 98.807 and only $245,000 in face value. The other bond has a 5.00 percent coupon at the same yield. Its price is 103.138, and it has a face value of $3,895,000. In addition, the small c next to the price indicates that it is callable, whereas the companion bond with the smaller coupon is not.

Often companion bonds (split-coupon bonds) like these are created for institutional and retail consumption. Retail buyers tend to be reluctant to buy bonds with large premiums. Frequently this occurs because the coupons are being consumed and the buyer is effectively spending part of her principal. Institutional customers, on the other hand, have a preference for the larger coupons because they help protect the bond from market discount taxes, which may be due on some discounts.

| 2026 | 245,000 | 4.50 | 4.60 | 98.807 | |
| 2026 | 3,895,000 | 5.00 | 4.60 | 103.138^c | |

Figure 4-8   Companion Bonds

A bond issued at a premium, an original issue premium (OIP), does not become a discount until the price falls below par. This bond's price can fall more than three points before the holder begins to feel the impact of market discount taxes.

The difference in par amounts is also consistent with the retail/institutional allocations. Institutions would probably not be interested in a new issue with an amount below $1,000,000.

The pattern of couponing is generally reflective of retail buying patterns. The retail companion bonds all have a 15-year or shorter maturity. It is not that retail investors never buy longer-term bonds, but that, as a group, their buying preference is clearly for shorter maturities. This issue also demonstrates that most of the par value sold occurs on the very longest maturities for revenue bonds.

This would be expected because the maturity of the borrowing approximately matches the expected life of the asset. A power plant should be financed with long-term bonds. Selling shorter-term bonds exposes the issuer to rollover risk as the short-term debt matures and the project needs to be refinanced. One would not issue bonds with maturities longer than the life of the asset because there would no longer be any revenue to pay the interest.

STRUCTURING GENERAL OBLIGATION AND REVENUE BONDS

There are many different ways to structure general obligation bonds (GOs) and revenue bonds, but it is useful to note some typical differences. Payments on GOs come from or are secured by the general fund of the issuer, whereas a pure revenue bond does not have general fund support. That does not mean that GOs are always the highest priority under the state's constitution. In California, for example, repayment of the GO debt comes ahead of all other state obligations with the exception of those for education.

GO issues typically need to be approved by the voters, whereas revenue bonds do not. In addition, GOs will often have shorter maturities than revenue bonds and employ level debt service so that the total of the coupon interest and the maturing principal is equal every year. The use of level debt service in GOs facilitates budgeting for the bond's repayment.

Looking again at our revenue bond example, we see that some of the serial bonds and all of the term bonds have calls. The issuer has an optional call beginning on January 1, 2019, as specified in the optional redemption section of the OS (see Figure 4-9).

The term bonds also have mandatory redemptions. Each has its own. Figure 4-10 shows the one for the 2032 bond.

The issuer has agreed to provide continuous updates on material changes to the data presented in the OS. This is shown in Figure 4-11. The issuer agrees to report monetary

Optional Redemption

The Series A Bonds maturing on and after July 1, 2019 will be subject to redemption prior to maturity at the option of the Department, in whole or in part, on any date on or after January 1, 2019 from any source of available funds, at a redemption price equal to the principal amount to be redeemed, plus accrued but unpaid interest to the redemption date, without premium.

Figure 4-9   Optional Calls

Mandatory Redemption

The Series A Bonds maturing on July 1, 2032, will be subject to mandatory redemption prior to maturity on July 1, 2031 and on each July 1 thereafter, from Sinking Fund Installments for such Series A Bonds, at a redemption price equal to the principal amount thereof, without premium, which Sinking Fund Installments for such Series A Bonds are to be made at the times and in the amounts sufficient to provide for the mandatory redemption of such Series A Bonds in the years and amounts set forth below:

Mandatory Redemption Date

(July 1)	Amount
2031	$5,350,000
2032	$5,630,000

Figure 4-10   Mandatory Calls

CONTINUING DISCLOSURE

The Department will . . . [provide] financial information and operating data relating to the Power System (the "Annual Report") by not later than 270 days following the end of the Department's fiscal year. . . . [N]otices of material events will be filed by the Department with the MSRB through the EMMA system.

Reporting of Significant Events
The Department shall give . . . notice of the occurrence of any of the following events. . . .

1. principal and interest payment delinquencies.
2. non-payment related defaults.
3. modifications to rights of the Owners of the Bonds.
4. optional, contingent or unscheduled Bond calls.
5. defeasances.
6. rating changes.
7. adverse tax opinions or events affecting the tax-exempt status of the Bonds.
8. unscheduled draws on the debt service reserves reflecting financial difficulties.
9. unscheduled draws on the credit enhancements reflecting financial difficulties.
10. substitution of the credit or liquidity providers or their failure to perform.
11. release, substitution or sale of property securing repayment of the Bonds.

Figure 4-11   Continuing Disclosure Items

and other defaults. Changes in the credit of the issuer, changes in the rights of the bondholders, and exercise of bond calls are to be reported. In addition, defeasances (which typically relate to refundings) will be disclosed.

RATINGS AND RECALIBRATIONS

The Great Recession led to the Great Recalibration of municipal bond ratings. Before the Great Recession in 2007–2009, ratings in the municipal bond market were a relatively simple matter. Each bond was assigned a letter grade based on its creditworthiness. The rater often displayed elements of judgment, focusing more on expected future events and less on historical default experiences.

In rough terms, the rating agencies follow a schema of prime, medium-grade, and speculative. Bonds rated as prime or medium-grade are said to be "investment grade." This satisfies certain regulatory constraints for buyers and broadens the demand for the bonds.

The three largest agencies, Moody's, Standard & Poor's (S&P), and Fitch, all assign the triple A rating, Aaa, AAA, and AAA, respectively, to the prime category. For cases where the issuer's credit is very strong but not prime, variations of Aa or AA are used. If a bond is given a rating in the category of Baa or BBB, depending on the agency, it shows that the credit is adequate. Ratings of Ba or BB going down to D indicate that the credit is viewed as speculative or in default. The symbol WD is used when the rating has been withdrawn, often reflecting a bad or deteriorating condition for the issuer.

If an issuer wants a rating, it will typically go to one or more of the established rating agencies—Moody's, S&P, or Fitch—but there is now a growing list of alternatives. The bond does not have to be rated at all, and it is the issuer who pays for the rating. Issuers will be tempted to shop around among the rating agencies to get the highest rating, something that the rating agencies wish to avoid because it puts them in competition with one another to provide the highest rating. The result is that the rating agencies tend to use very similar standards in assigning ratings, and most ratings are quite close to one another. If rating agencies give different ratings, such as A from one agency and AA from another, the issuer has received a *split rating*.

Many Bond Types

The municipal bond market is widely dispersed in terms of size, region, and use of funds. There are about 10,000 to 14,000 issues a year with average sizes of $25 to $35 million. The issuer is going to seek out a rating only if it thinks it is going to get a relatively good one. As a result, many speculative bonds are not rated. In addition, the rating that the issuer gets must save enough in the borrowing cost to cover the cost of the rating. All these factors result in many smaller issues not being rated and there being little continuing information about them from ratings updates.

Just because an issue is small does not mean that it is unsuitable as an investment. In the absence of a rating, however, investors may have to take it upon themselves to monitor the fiscal condition of the borrower, which can be both expensive and difficult even if the issuer supplies EMMA updates. Alternatively, the investor can use the professional management skills of a fund manager.

Until the subprime mortgage crisis, about 60 percent of the new issues in the municipal bond market were insured by one of a handful of municipal bond insurers. These, in turn, were all rated by the rating agencies at their highest level. Insured bonds were given the rating of the insurer, not the issuer. This caused most of the newly issued bonds in the municipal bond market to be rated triple A.

The insurers, it turned out, held a large proportion of their assets in subprime or other risky mortgage-backed securities. When these assets failed, the bond insurers suffered calamitous economic losses, with the result that they are now, in general, no longer effective insurers. Currently only one insurance company is very active in the new issue market, and it is not rated triple A. It insures around 5 percent of the new issue market.

Market Restructures

The demise of the insurance industry radically altered the credit-rating profile in the municipal market. As a practical matter, investors now can rely only on the credit of the issuer, the underlying credit in an insured deal.

Certain anomalies in the process of rating municipal bonds also became apparent. First, the insurance standard that the insurers had used was usually "zero loss." Under this standard, only bonds that were never expected to default were insured.

Since there were very few defaults on the insured municipal bonds, one may wonder why the bonds themselves weren't rated AAA to begin with. It seems that only bonds that didn't need insurance were insured. And because insurers incurred few, if any, defaults on their municipal bond program, it was a very profitable business.

The low number of defaults on insured bonds happened in spite of the fact that the insurers were insuring the majority of bonds being sold in the municipal market in some years. It was clear that ratings on municipal bonds were systematically lower than those in other rated sectors, such as the corporate bond sector. The lower ratings on municipal bonds forced issuers to pay higher yields, or sell their bonds more cheaply, than comparably rated corporations.

Issuers Complain

The issuers began to object vehemently. California Treasurer Bill Lockyer was especially vocal in 2008, demanding that ratings he considered to be "unfair" be changed. For professionals in the municipal bond market, however, this was old news. In 2002, Moody's had published an extensive Special Comment on defaults in the municipal market. The comment studied municipal bonds rated by Moody's from 1970 through 2000. It found that 18 long-term bonds had defaulted; most of these were bonds of not-for-profit hospitals. Among general obligation bonds and essential-purpose revenue bonds like water and sewer bonds, no defaults were observed. The 10-year cumulative default rate on all municipal bonds was 0.0043 percent, compared with 0.675 percent for AAA-rated corporate bonds. For the municipal bonds that defaulted, the bondholders on average recovered 66 percent of their par value, versus 42 percent for defaulted corporate bonds.

In spite of the obviously superior credit performance of municipals, Moody's had given municipals their own lower

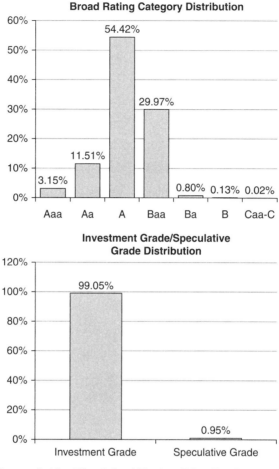

Figure 4-12   Municipal Rating Distribution, 1970–2000 (*Source:* Moody's Investors Service.)

rating scale. Only about 3 percent of the bonds were rated Aaa on their own, without any insurance. See Figure 4-12. The other rating agencies would have had distributions consistent with this, since they were, to a large extent, rating exactly the same population of issuers using roughly the same standards.

Dodd-Frank Reforms

The rating issue eventually reached a resolution in the passage of the Dodd-Frank Wall Street Reform and Consumer Protection Act on July 21, 2010. This is a voluminous piece of legislation, only a small portion of which deals with the rating agencies. Even that, however, is extensive. The legislation specifically addresses nationally recognized statistical rating organizations (NRSROs), which includes Moody's, S&P, and Fitch as well as others, making them subject to the legislation.

Congress was especially concerned about the inherent conflict of interest involved in having an issuer buy its own rating. Under the legislation, raters of issuers are not allowed to be consultants to issuers whose securities they rate. Individuals who rate bonds are required to be reported to the SEC in the event that they are subsequently hired by an entity that they rated. The regulatory agencies were instructed to create new rules to implement the intent of Congress within a year of the bill's enactment.

The rating agencies were required to clearly define the meanings of any of their rating symbols and to use them consistently. Importantly, for municipal bonds, the rating agencies were required to establish procedures calculating the probability of an issuer's default or its failure to make payments.

Congress definitely wanted to reduce the importance of the current rating entities in the law. Federal agencies and regulators are instructed to delete references to specific ratings from their rules.

Municipal credit analysts had been reluctant to fundamentally change the way in which they viewed their analysis. Traditionally, municipal bonds were evaluated relative to other municipal bonds on a variety of factors. This process, though, led to significantly lower ratings for municipals than for comparable taxable securities because the analysts wanted to magnify the differences among the many high-quality issuers in the municipal market. They feared that if the municipal issuers were rated like corporations, their ratings would be bunched at the very top end of the rating scale. So, the mean rating for municipal bonds was pegged lower than it would be for corporate bonds, and the municipal bond ratings were spread out across a wider range of rating categories.

Municipal bonds did receive systematically lower ratings. Lower ratings tend to increase borrowing costs for issuers. This process led to the creation of externalities in which rating decisions had spillover effects by imposing additional costs on politically sensitive entities, even if they were very good credits. If an issuer was rated AA on the municipal bond scale but would be AAA on the corporate scale, it would typically pay 0.20 percent more in interest on its debt. The industry and particularly the rating agencies eventually responded by harmonizing municipal bond ratings with those of other rating groups.

Ratings Raised

This process of placing municipal and corporate ratings on an equal footing, based primarily upon expected defaults, required that a great many municipal bonds have their ratings increased. Reducing the ratings of corporate bonds was clearly impractical, since it would have triggered many credit events.

Increases in municipal bond ratings happened at a time when state and local governments were suffering significant budget problems, and this, of course, seemed peculiar to many investors. Nevertheless, it was clear to the rating agencies by 2010 that it was necessary to recalibrate the municipal bond rating scale to make it consistent with corporate bond ratings. Municipal ratings were changed to use the same standards that corporate issuers faced.

The change in Fitch ratings was illustrative. General obligations of states or local governments that formerly were rated A+ or higher on the old muni scale were raised a single notch. Thus, the rating on an A+ rated GO was revised to AA–. State and local GOs rated BBB– to A were raised two notches. Water, sewer, and public power bonds were treated like GOs. Other ratings were adjusted on a case-by-case basis.

Fitch's treatment of water, sewer, and power bonds is instructive. These are "essential-purpose" revenue bonds. Unlike general obligation bonds, the funds to repay them do not come from taxing sources, but rather from specific revenues derived from the sale or processing of water, sewer, and power. Because what they produce is essential for the functioning of a governmental unit like a city, they are often treated like general obligation bonds of an issuer for credit purposes. And, essential-purpose revenue bonds of high-quality issuers may be considered to be superior in credit to the general obligation bonds of riskier issuers.

Few Rated Defaults

On March 12, 2012, Fitch released a study of defaults based on more than 22,000 long-term unenhanced bond issues with a value of approximately $1 trillion. The study ran from 1999 through 2011. It covered a broad spectrum of municipal issuers, including states and state authorities, cities, counties, school districts, special districts, water and sewer districts, toll road authorities, airports, private educational organizations, cultural organizations, senior living organizations, and healthcare organizations. The average default rate was 0.04 percent through 2011.

In fact, a Fitch study issued on March 25, 2011, showed that in the years of the Great Recession, 2007 and 2008, a total of three Fitch-rated bonds defaulted. That Fitch study showed the effects of the rating recalibration that had occurred. Fitch's recalibration resulted in 64 percent of the ratings being revised upward. Ratings were also changed independent of the recalibration, and these downgrades, as expected after a recession, occurred more frequently than upgrades. Other than that, ratings were generally stable.

We can learn more from the 2012 Fitch study, however, by comparing the distribution of recalibrated ratings with the rating distribution we saw from Moody's in Figure 4-12. There the majority of the ratings are A. By the time of the Fitch study covering the next 10 years, however, the typical rating had migrated to AA, as Table 4-1 shows.

As you can see, only 2 percent of municipal bonds are rated below investment grade by Fitch; this is representative

Table 4-1   Fitch Distribution of Ratings, 2011

Fitch Rating	Percentage of Total
AAA	13%
AA	50%
A	27%
BBB	8%
Below investment grade	2%

Source: Fitch Ratings.

of the industry. The generally high credit quality of municipal bonds is one reason. In addition, as we indicated earlier, there is self-selection. An issuer will seek a rating only when it expects to get a relatively good one.

But, there are other reasons for the high ratings, as well. Numerous levels of government may intervene to preserve weaker credits. This helps prevent any contagion effect in a state. New Orleans is an example, where the state and federal governments acted to aid local agencies to alleviate the hurricane disaster and continue the functioning of the city.

Importantly, issuers who know that they are in trouble may refuse to supply enough data to the rating agency to allow it to properly assess the financial condition of the credit. In that case, it is likely that the credit rating will be withdrawn altogether (WD).

For investors who are looking for "junk" municipal bonds, this issuer behavior is a cautionary flag. Below-investment-grade bonds require careful and continuous monitoring, since the usual sources of financial information about an issuer may be unavailable. Municipal issuers are not required to file the usual 8-K and 10-K reports like their corporate counterparts. As a result, the data on the financial condition of the entities may be restricted to individuals "in the know."

The 2012 Fitch report also provides information on defaults by rating. Not surprisingly, defaults were concentrated in the lower-rated bonds. While there were few defaults overall, there also were few non-investment-grade ratings, and a surprisingly large number of these bonds defaulted. Over one, five, and ten years, the percentages of non-investment-grade bonds that defaulted were 1.93 percent, 7.85 percent, and 17.57 percent, respectively. The corresponding default rates for investment-grade issues were 0.01 percent, 0.08 percent, and 0.29 percent.

Ratings Stable

Finally, the Fitch study can provide us with some idea of the stability of ratings. In general, municipal bond ratings are quite stable, but higher-rated bonds have more stable ratings than lower-rated bonds. We can see this in Table 4-2,

Table 4-2   Average Annual Transition Rates, 1999–2010

Rating at the Beginning of the Year	Percent with the Same Rating at the End of the Year
AAA	98.74%
AA	96.68%
A	91.30%
BBB	90.23%
BB	84.92%
B	78.50%
CCC to C	79.07%

Source: Fitch Ratings.

which shows the average annual transition of ratings from 1999 to 2010. The ratings of the highest-rated bonds, AAA-rated bonds, are especially stable. On average, more than 98 percent of the time, a bond that started the year at AAA ended the year at AAA. At the other end of the spectrum, if the bond is rated CCC to C, it retained that rating only 79 percent of the time. Of course, some of these lower-rated bonds may have been upgraded rather than downgraded.

The ratings are reviewed by analysts with reasonable frequency after the bond is initially sold. These reviews are typically annual unless the analyst is aware of unusual events affecting the issuer. The rating analysts, however, are likely to report only on rating changes. When the rating is not changed, it will be "affirmed."

Ratings Can Surprise

Occasionally there is a ratings surprise for a municipal bond issuer, but these are quite infrequent. Jefferson County, Alabama, was a relatively recent example of such a rating surprise. The case was highly unusual and involved elements of fraud.

Nevertheless, municipal bonds are not default-free. Investors should diversify their holdings to protect against surprises having an undue effect on their overall portfolios. In addition, if a bond is not rated and the investor lacks regular access to updated information about the issuer, the bond is probably not an appropriate investment.

Rating trends should also be observed. A steady trend of downgrades to an issuer is a clear signal that trouble may be ahead. Reserve fund draws are also a red flag. Unusually large short-term borrowings should also be questioned. But absolute and universal rules are often difficult to apply, given the wide range of bonds and borrowers.

Finally, it is important to distinguish bankruptcies from defaults. Both are rare in the municipal bond market, but defaults do not necessarily imply bankruptcies. And even if the bond payments do get rescheduled, the bondholders ordinarily do get paid. Total losses in the Depression amounted to about 1/2 percent of the face value of outstanding bonds, even though there were thousands of defaults. Many defaults are technical in nature, resulting from the issuer's not adhering to some of the covenants in the bond deal. These can be and most often are cured.

Defaults on interest and principal payments occur occasionally and are concentrated in a few sectors of the market, particularly tax increment and healthcare bonds. Careful research in these sectors can be expected to materially reduce the chance of default in a portfolio.

5

Conduit Financing

Now we can compare the standard revenue bond that we examined in the previous chapter with a conduit financing. In the LADWP bond in the previous chapter, the money went to the Department of Water and Power, a public agency. Here we will see the proceeds of the bond issue going to a private company, even though it is a tax-exempt municipal bond.

Conduit financings are also revenue bonds, but the official public borrower is not the source of the repayment on the bonds. This is often confusing for investors because the same "conduit" issuer can be selling bonds on behalf of many different borrowers with very different credits.

Conduit bonds can have the same public issuer but many different private entities. The buyer needs to look through the conduit to find the real borrower, the private entity.

These conduit financings allow private entities to borrow in the municipal bond market as a matter of public policy.

$227,160,000
ARIZONA HEALTH FACILITIES AUTHORITY
Revenue Bonds
(Banner Health)
Series 2008A

Figure 5-1   Title of the Issue

The borrowings may be for pollution control or health-care, for example, or other socially redeeming activities. The essential point here is for the investors to recognize that the loan they are making is to a private firm and not a public entity. If they would not lend to the private firm directly, they should not buy the conduit bonds. If they would make the loan directly, they may want to invest in the conduit bonds, subject to price and structure.

In this case, we will look at an issue sold by the Arizona Health Facilities Authority, which is one of many conduit bonds in the municipal bond market. The title of the bond from the OS is shown in Figure 5-1.

The loan is for $227,160,000 in face value. Arizona Health Facilities Authority is the official borrower. The bonds are clearly marked as revenue bonds and with the name Banner Health. It is Banner Health that investors need to understand.

The summary of the legal opinion at the top of the first page of the OS is a standard tax-exempt municipal bond summary (see Figure 5-2). The bonds are federally tax-exempt: "interest . . . is excluded from gross income." And the bonds are not a "preference item" and so are not AMT bonds.

Figure 5-3 shows the use of proceeds for the issue. The funds raised by selling the bond issue will be used by the private corporation to retire a bridge loan.

In the opinion of Hawkins Delafield & Wood LLB Bond Counsel to the Issuer, under existing statutes and court decisions and assuming continuing compliance with certain tax covenants described herein, (i) interest on the Series 2008A Bonds is excluded from gross income for Federal income tax purposes pursuant to Section 103 of the Internal Revenue Code of 1986, as amended (the "Code"), and (ii) interest on the Series 2008A Bonds is not treated as a preference item in calculating the alternative minimum tax imposed on individuals and corporations under the Code; such interest, however, is included in the adjusted current earnings of certain corporations for purposes of calculating the alternative minimum tax imposed on such corporations.

Figure 5-2   Legal Opinion

In the issuer section of the official statement, we see that the issuer, the Arizona Health Facilities Authority, has no taxing authority and no funds to repay the bonds. This is made clear in Figure 5-4. The bonds are not a debt of the official issuer, the state of Arizona, or any political subdivision of the state.

If the bondholder has any doubts about what is meant by a conduit, he should read the description of the issuer in detail (see Figure 5-5). The issuer is an entity created by the state to sell bonds to finance healthcare facilities. It has no funds to repay the bonds and no staff. It will not monitor the private entity that is using the funds, the obligated group.

If the issuer is not responsible for the debt, who is? The obligor. In this case, the bondholders should look to the

The proceeds of the sale of the Series 2008A Bonds will be used to (i) refinance the outstanding principal amount of a $224,225,000 bridge loan (the "Bridge Loan") plus accrued interest thereon from JPMorgan Chase Bank, N.A. to the Corporation pursuant to a Bridge Loan Agreement dated as of April 1, 2008.

Figure 5-3   Use of Proceeds

THE SERIES 2008A BONDS DO NOT REPRESENT OR CONSTITUTE A DEBT OF THE ISSUER, THE STATE OF ARIZONA OR ANY POLITICAL SUBDIVISION THEREOF WITHIN THE MEANING OF THE PROVISIONS OF THE CONSTITUTION OR STATUTES OF THE STATE OF ARIZONA OR A PLEDGE OF THE FAITH AND CREDIT OF THE ISSUER, THE STATE OF ARIZONA OR ANY POLITICAL SUBDIVISION THEREOF. THE ISSUANCE OF THE SERIES 2008A BONDS DOES NOT OBLIGATE, IN ANY WAY, THE ISSUER, THE STATE OF ARIZONA OR ANY POLITICAL SUBDIVISION THEREOF TO LEVY ANY TAXES OR APPROPRIATE ANY FUNDS FOR THE PAYMENT OF THE PRINCIPAL THEREOF OR THE INTEREST OR ANY PREMIUM ON THE SERIES 2008A BONDS. THE ISSUER HAS NO TAXING POWER.

Figure 5-4   No Taxing Authority

THE ISSUER

The Issuer is a political subdivision and instrumentality of the State of Arizona (the "State") established pursuant to the provisions of the Constitution of the State and Title 36, Chapter 4.2, Arizona Revised Statutes, as amended (the "Act"). The Issuer is governed by a Board of Directors, consisting of seven members who are appointed by the Governor of the State. Pursuant to the Act, the Issuer is empowered to issue bonds for the purposes, among other things, of providing financing and refinancing for the acquisition, construction, equipping and improvement of certain health care facilities.

The Issuer has no taxing power and no source of funds for payment of the Series 2008A Bonds other than the underlying contractual obligations made by or on behalf of the Obligated Group. The Issuer does not have the power to pledge the general credit or taxing power of the State or of any political subdivision thereof.

Except for an executive director, the Issuer does not employ any staff to carry out its limited functions and contracts with independent third parties to do so. The Issuer does not and will not in the future monitor the financial condition of the Obligated Group or the operation of the Project, or otherwise monitor payment of the Series 2008A Bonds or compliance with the documents relating thereto. The responsibility for the operation of the Project will rest entirely with the Obligated Group and not with the Issuer. The Issuer will rely entirely upon the Bond Trustee and the Obligated Group to carry out their responsibilities under the Loan Agreement and with respect to the Project. The Issuer has assets and may attain additional assets in the future. However, such assets are not pledged to secure payment of the Series 2008A Bonds and the Issuer has no obligation nor expectation of making such assets subject to the lien of the Bond Indenture.

Figure 5-5   Description of the Issuer

Banner Health is an Arizona nonprofit corporation and a tax-exempt organization described in Section 501(c)(3) of the Internal Revenue Code of 1986, as amended (the "Code"). The Corporation is one of the largest secular nonprofit health care systems in the United States. The Corporation owns, leases or manages 19 acute care hospitals in seven states with a total of approximately 3,060 licensed acute care beds and 231 behavioral and rehabilitation licensed beds; one behavioral health facility in Arizona with approximately 96 licensed behavioral beds; three facilities (including acute care hospitals with licensed long-term care beds) in two states providing nursing care services with a total of approximately 208 licensed long-term care beds; and 37 skilled nursing licensed beds at two acute care hospitals. The Corporation also operates home health agencies, nursing registries, clinics and home medical equipment supply services.

Figure 5-6   Description of the Obligor

"obligated group," essentially the healthcare corporation, which is a charity under Section 501(c) (3) of the Internal Revenue Code. This is made clear in Figure 5-6.

The bonds have the usual optional and mandatory calls. In addition, however, there is an extraordinary optional call (EOP) described in Figure 5-7. If the facilities financed by the bond issue are destroyed or condemned, the bonds will be called at par ("without premium") from the insurance proceeds or condemnation award.

Extraordinary Optional Redemption. The Series 2008A Bonds are subject to redemption prior to their stated maturity, at the option of the Corporation . . . on any date, from hazard insurance or condemnation proceeds received with respect to the facilities financed or refinanced . . . at a Redemption Price equal to the principal amount thereof, plus accrued interest to the date fixed for redemption, without premium.

Figure 5-7   Extraordinary Calls

The Series 2008A Bonds are also subject to redemption prior to their stated maturity at the option of the Corporation . . . without premium, if, as a result of any changes in the Constitution of the United States of America or any state, or legislative or administrative action or inaction by the United States of America or any state, or any agency or political subdivision thereof, or by reason of any judicial decisions there is a good faith determination by the Corporation that (a) the Loan Agreement or the Master Indenture has become void or unenforceable or impossible to perform or (b) unreasonable burdens or excessive liabilities have been imposed on the Corporation, including, without limitation, federal, state or other ad valorem property, income or other taxes not being imposed on the date of the Bond Indenture.

Figure 5-8   Tax Calls

The bond is also expressly subject to being called if adverse legal events, including excessive new taxes, occur. See Figure 5-8.

6

Refundings

Another way to classify municipal bonds is as new money versus refunding. A bond issue is new money if the amount borrowed is used for any purpose except retiring other debt. In Figure 6-1, we can see the total amount of municipal bonds issued by states and local governments since 1996. In a typical year, about one-third of the issuance is for refunding and the remaining two-thirds is for new money. For example, in 2010, $443 billion in total issuance came into the municipal bond market, which was a record. Of this amount, $153 billion was refunding or combined refunding and new money. In 2011, however, the expiration of the tax subsidy bond program Build America Bonds (BABs), along with state and local financial difficulties, has led to a precipitous decline in issuance. Bond sales fell to $287 billion, of which almost half was refunding or combined issuance.

In the parlance of the market, a project is "funded" when money is borrowed to pay for a road, building, or other

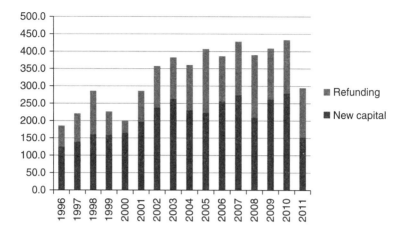

Figure 6-1   Refundings and New Capital by Year (billions of dollars) (*Source:* Securities Industry and Financial Markets Association.)

structure. If money is again borrowed to finance the same project and the original bond is in some way retired, the second bond is said to be a refunding bond. Thus, the issuer sells a new issue called the refunding bond and uses the money from that issue to retire the previously outstanding issue, the refunded bond.

The IRS defines a refunding very broadly: "A refunding issue is an issue of obligations the proceeds of which are used to pay principal of, or interest or redemption price on, another issue of bonds."

CURRENT REFUNDINGS

Refundings can be of two different types: current and advance. In a current refunding, the new bond issue is sold within 90 days of retiring the old bond issue. In general, a bond can be retired either because it has matured or because the issuer has exercised a call provision. Here we will assume that the old bond is retired because of a call provision.

As we saw in previous chapters, a call can be either mandatory or optional. In a mandatory call, the issuer is obliged to call and retire all or a prescribed amount of the bond on a specific date that was spelled out in the indenture and the official statement (OS). A bond with a mandatory call will have its call funded. That is, the money used to call the bonds away from the holders in a mandatory bond call will be accumulated over time in a *sinking fund*. Failure to make payments into the sinking fund is a type of bond default and is subject to disclosure. An issuer who is not making the required sinking fund payments is sending a strong signal to investors that there may be serious financial problems afoot.

An optional call provision gives the issuer the choice of when, if at all, to call the bonds away from the bondholders. The call provisions are spelled out in the official statement. An issuer has no inherent right to call a bond. The issuer buys the right by paying higher yields on the bond issue.

If an optional call is exercised, the price plus accrued interest must be paid to the bondholder along with any call premium. A call premium is the amount by which the call price exceeds par. If there is a call premium, it generally declines to zero over time. The bondholder should expect that the exercise of an optional call will benefit the issuer to the detriment of the bondholder. This detriment is normally the opportunity cost of having to replace the called bond with bonds in the market that offer lower yields.

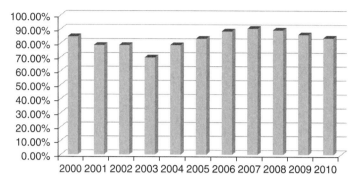

Figure 6-2   Percentage of Long-Term Bonds Issued with Optional Calls (*Source:* Securities Industry and Financial Markets Association.)

Optional calls are very common in the municipal bond market. Figure 6-2 shows that in a typical year, between 80 and 90 percent of all new issues contain optional calls. Not all of these are exercised, but nevertheless investors should be very aware that, especially in a declining-interest-rate market, the issuers may call their bonds away from them and refinance the old bonds with lower-cost refunding bonds. The bondholders whose bonds are called away are not, of course, required to purchase the refunding bonds.

There is a market convention for structuring optional calls that we saw in some of the bonds we examined in earlier chapters. Usually for a period in the life of a long-term bond, the call is not operational. In a bond with a 30-year maturity, for instance, the bond will ordinarily not be callable during the first 10 years; in this case, it is said to be "call protected" or to have 10 years of call protection. After the first 10 years pass, the bond can be called, generally on any interest payment date. The bond is then "currently callable."

The structure of the call is at the discretion of the issuer, and wide arrays of different types of calls exist. Municipal housing bonds, for example, are issued by state and local housing authorities. The lending standards for these bonds have always been solid, so these bonds have not experienced the same degree of problems as taxable housing bonds. There are no subprime municipal bonds, even though these bonds can be structured as pass-through bonds or broken up into tranches with different effective maturities. These bonds are backed by pools of mortgages, and as the borrowers prepay those mortgages, the municipal housing bonds will experience periodic calls.

The convention for the call price for fixed-coupon bonds used to be 102 declining to 100. The value above 100 is called a *call premium*. So when the bond is callable at a price of 102, it has a 2 percent call premium. Call premiums have declined systematically over the last several years, and now the typical new issue has no call premium.

Zero-coupon bonds and their cousins the compound accretion bonds (CABs) are also typically callable. In that case, the call price is a percentage of the accreted price. If the bond is sold at a new issue yield of 5 percent, its accreted price after issuance is the price that the bond would have at that yield. Suppose the bond initially sold for a price of 90. A year later, its accreted price may be 91. The call price might be 101 percent of 91. This is an example, of course. The actual call schedule, if any, for a zero-coupon bond will be spelled out in the OS.

REASONS FOR REFUNDINGS

There are a number of reasons why an issuer would engage in a refunding:

- *Interest-rate savings.* If interest rates have declined or the issuer's credit has improved, the cost to the issuer, including the expenses of the new issue, may be lower than the cost of the old issue.
- *Debt restructuring.* In a refunding, the new issue may extend the issuer's maturity profile.
- *Change of covenants.* The old agreement on the refunded bond is retired when the bond is retired. As a result, any adverse covenants that may have been negotiated in the first issue are removed. What this really means is that when the original bond issue was sold, the issuer may have agreed to limitations on new issues and other covenants. The issuer may wish to eliminate these agreements contained in the older bonds, either because it has established better credit or because in the current market environment, the covenants aren't required anymore.

ADVANCE REFUNDINGS

If the purchase of the refunded bond is delayed for more than 90 days after the refunding bond is sold, the IRS considers the bond to be an "advance refunding bond." These are also referred to as advanced refunding bonds or prerefunding bonds, and they are largely a peculiarity of the tax-exempt market.

Advance refunding bonds have been a matter of special concern for the IRS for many years. They are legal, but they are highly regulated to prevent the issuers from engaging in arbitrage between the taxable and tax-exempt markets.

In the typical advance refunding transaction, the refunded bond is not retired. Instead, the money obtained from selling the refunding bond is, in a sense, deposited in an escrow account at the bank. The principal and interest earned on the investment of the refunding bond proceeds are used to pay off the old issue. The holder of the refunded bond can look only to the investments purchased with the refunding proceeds for payment, not the issuer. The refunding issue is paid off by the issuer.

Because the investment at the bank is paying off the old bond, the old bond gets a new credit that is often better than the credit of the original issuer. This may result in a price appreciation on the bonds. In practice, the advance refunding transaction generally qualifies as a legal defeasance. If a liability is legally defeased, it is no longer considered to be an obligation of the issuer. The issuer does not have to pay the debt service on the refunded bonds. In addition to that, the defeased bond is no longer recorded on the books of the issuer for accounting purposes.

There is another type of advance refunding besides a defeasance advance refunding. It is called a *crossover advance refunding*. In a crossover advance refunding, the money from selling a new refunding issue is also placed with the bank in an escrow account that buys interest-bearing securities. Unlike in a defeasance advance refunding, however, where the escrow account immediately becomes the sole source of payment of the debt service on the old refunded bond, in a crossover refunding, the escrow pays the debt service on the new refunding bond.

In a crossover refunding, the new issue funds its own debt service until the call date of the old bond. On the refunded bond's call date, money from the escrow at the bank is used to call the old bond, and the issuer crosses over and starts to pay the interest on the new refunding bond.

With a defeasance advance refunding, the credit of the outstanding refunded bond changes from that of the issuer to that of the bonds in the escrow. With a crossover refunding, the credit of the outstanding bond remains the same because the issuer continues to pay on the bond. The credit of the refunding bond in a crossover refunding remains that of the escrow established with the money from the sale of the refunding bond. At the crossover date, the refunded bond is called and retired, and the new refunding bond becomes a liability of the issuer.

Most advance refundings are defeasance advance refundings, but both types are sold. The choice between them depends most importantly on the amount of savings that either will produce for the issuer. Different IRS rules apply to each. From here on, we will assume that we are dealing with defeasance advance refundings.

Advance refundings are subject to a myriad of IRS regulations and rules. First, the IRS makes a distinction between governmental-activity bonds (also called public-purpose bonds) and private-activity bonds (private-purpose bonds). Generally, if a significant amount of the bond issue's proceeds is used for the purposes of private organizations or individuals, the bond is a private-activity bond. For example, bonds sold for the construction of a city hall are governmental-activity bonds because the public owns and uses the facility. Bonds sold to build a for-profit factory are private-activity bonds, not because a factory isn't a worthy cause, but because a private corporation owns it.

Only governmental-activity bonds can be advance refunded, and governmental-activity bonds can be advance refunded only once. Prior to the current crop of advance refunding rules, an issuer could advance refund bonds that had themselves been advance refunded. Now an issuer is not allowed to advance refund an advance refunding bond.

In addition, the escrow that the refunding creates must be set up to call and retire the refunded bond at the first available date. In prior years, without this rule, the escrow was often structured to pay off the refunded bond at maturity. Logically, these were called escrowed to maturity bonds, or ETMs.

The amount of interest that the issuer can earn on the investments from the refunding bonds is also restricted. The basic idea is that the IRS does not allow the earnings on investments in taxable bonds that were made with the money borrowed through a tax-exempt refunding bond to be materially greater than the interest cost (the yield) paid on the refunding bonds.

If the issuer earns more on an investment than it pays to borrow the funds, there is positive arbitrage. Issuers are required to calculate the amount of arbitrage the bond earns and to rebate the earnings to the federal government every five years during the life of the bond.

While positive arbitrage is prohibited, negative arbitrage is not. It is not unusual for the investments in the escrow fund to earn less than the interest due on the refunding bond. It's easy to see how this can happen with positively sloped yield curves, where yields on long-term bonds are higher than those on shorter-term bonds. Consider a recently issued 30-year bond with a 10-year call. If it were to be advance refunded, it would have to be refunded to call, that is, in 10 years. The money from the refunding bond is paid to an escrow dedicated to the repayment of the refunded bond. Under current IRS rules, the escrow must usually be established to call and retire the bonds as soon as they are callable.

To borrow the money to create the escrow fund, a new long-term refunding bond must be sold. Suppose that it is sold at a 4.5 percent tax-exempt yield, but the investments can earn a taxable 10-year rate of only around 3.1 percent because that is the rate available in the market. The difference between a long-term tax-exempt rate and a shorter-term Treasury rate is negative 1.4 percent.

This difference is referred to as the *negative arbitrage* in the refunding. Negative arbitrage reduces the profitability of an advance refunding, sometimes dramatically. Negative arbitrage is one reason why high-coupon municipal bonds are often not advance refunded even though they are callable.

The savings to the issuer in an advance refunding are the discounted difference between the debt service of the old bond and the debt service of the new bond, reduced by negative arbitrage and issuing costs. Usually, the coupon on the refunded bond must be around 1 to 2 percent higher than that on the refunding bond in order to generate enough savings to justify the refunding. Even if the coupon differences between refunding and refunded bonds were large enough because of a bond market rally, the negative arbitrage in the market has prevented many advance refundings in the last several years.

Another reason for high-coupon bonds not being current or advance refunded with lower-coupon new issues of refunding bonds is their size. Many municipal issues have small par amounts. If the issue is smaller than about $10 million in total, even a large percentage change in coupons may not generate enough cash to cover the issuing costs. Each case, however, is different.

THE PRE-RE MARKET

The old refunded bond is payable solely from the interest and principal of the investment at the bank. The "bank" in this case is actually an escrow fund and normally contains high-grade investments such as U.S. Treasuries. The interest earnings and principal payments on the escrow fund exactly match the debt service requirements on the refunded bond. The refunded bond is normally rerated to triple A and receives a new CUSIP.

These advance refunded bonds are usually more homogeneous than most municipal bonds and have their own market segment—the pre-refunded bond market. In the trade they are called "pre-res" and are also referred to as "pre-reed" bonds.

Investors in pre-refunded bonds must investigate the exact composition of the escrows backing the bonds before they buy the bonds. While the convention is to fund the escrow with Treasuries, escrows often contain U.S. government agencies and other types of bonds. Unless the pre-re has 100 percent Treasuries, it will trade at a discount to a clean 100 percent Treasury-backed pre-re. And depending on how Washington handles its current deficit, there may be investors who will find even clean pre-res to be unsuitable investments.

Example of Pre-Re

In order to illustrate the structure of an advance refunded bond, we will take an example from EMMA. Here we look at a Heartland Consumers Power issue. In Figure 6-3, we see

ESCROW DEPOSIT AGREEMENT

Between

HEARTLAND CONSUMERS POWER DISTRICT

and

THE FIRST NATIONAL BANK IN SIOUX FALLS.,
as Escrow Agent

Dated as of June 1, 2011

Figure 6-3 Sample Escrow Agreement

the escrow deposit for the pre-re. The escrow deposit agreement is between a tax-exempt power bond issuer and a bank.

In Figure 6-4, we see selected paragraphs from the agreement. Bonds issued in 1992 are to be advance refunded

WHEREAS, a portion of the Series 1992 Bonds are currently outstanding and

 Heartland desires to provide for the advance refunding of certain of the Series 1992 Bonds maturing January 1, 2012 and January 1, 2017 (the "Refunded Bonds")

 WHEREAS, in order to provide a portion of the moneys necessary for the above stated purposes and for other purposes, Heartland will issue its $11,350,000 Electric System Second Lien Revenue Bonds, Series 2011 . . . adopted by Heartland's Board of Directors on June 13, 2011 (the "Bond Resolution"). . . .

 Section 2. Creation of Escrow Deposit Fund. There is hereby created and established with the Escrow Agent a special and irrevocable escrow designated the "2011 Heartland Escrow Deposit Fund" (the "Escrow Deposit Fund") to be held in the custody of the Escrow Agent separate and apart from other funds of Heartland or of the Escrow Agent. The Escrow Deposit Fund will contain moneys, to be deposited therein as provided in Section 3 hereof, which will be applied in accordance with said Section 3 to the purchase of the Government Securities, the principal of and interest on which will, according to calculations verified by Causey Demgen & Moore Inc., independent certified public accountants, be sufficient to pay the principal of and interest on the Refunded Bonds coming due up to and including their maturity dates, as provided in Section 4 hereof.

 Section 3. Funding of the Escrow Deposit Fund; Purchase of Government Securities. Concurrently with the execution of this Escrow Deposit Agreement, Heartland has deposited with the Escrow Agent and the Escrow Agent has received immediately available moneys in the amount of $11,325,578.61 from the proceeds of the Series 2011 Bonds.

 Concurrently with such deposits, the Escrow Agent shall apply $11,023,959.26 of such moneys described in the preceding sentence to the purchase of the Government Securities described in Schedule A attached hereto, with the remainder to be held uninvested as cash. The Escrow Agent shall deposit and hold such Government Securities in the Escrow Deposit Fund for application in accordance with Section 4 hereof.

 Section 4. Irrevocable Escrow; Application of Escrow Deposit Fund. The deposit of Government Securities in this Escrow Deposit Fund, as provided in Section 3 hereof, shall constitute an irrevocable deposit of said Government Securities, together with any interest earned thereon, for the benefit of the holders of the Refunded Bonds. Said Government Securities, together with any interest earned thereon, shall be held in escrow and shall be applied solely to the payment of principal of and the interest on the Refunded Bonds coming due up to and including their maturity (or, in the case of the Refunded Bonds maturing January 1, 2017, the sinking fund payment dates), in accordance with the debt service schedule.

Figure 6-4   Selected Portions of Escrow Agreement

under this 2011 agreement. The power agency will issue $11,350,000 of refunding bonds. Section 2 of the agreement obligates the issuer to use the money to create an escrow fund. In Section 3, we see that $11,023,959.26 will be used to purchase government bonds. Section 4 makes it clear that the money will be used only to pay off the old bonds.

7

Elements of Taxation

In this chapter, we will concern ourselves with bonds that are federally tax-exempt under Internal Revenue Code (IRC) Section 103. There are now many taxable municipal bonds as well. As always, investors should consult their own tax advisors when considering the tax and accounting treatments of a particular bond.

CONGRESS CAN TAX MUNIS

The first place to begin the discussion of the municipal bond tax exemption is with the power of Congress to tax municipal bonds. The states and the federal government have engaged in a form of reciprocity with regard to taxation. For example, Congress does not tax the earnings of state enterprises like water departments, and the states don't impose property taxes on the post offices.

This notion of reciprocity was extended to the interest on both the states' and the U.S. Treasury's bonds. The states don't tax the interest on bonds issued by the U.S. Treasury, and the Treasury doesn't tax the interest on municipal bonds.

Through much of the last century, the municipal market believed that the exemption of municipal bond interest from federal income tax was constitutionally based. This argument relied on explanatory language in an 1895 case, *Pollock v. Farmers' Loan & Trust Co*, 157 U.S. 429, to the effect that the power to tax was the power to destroy. This, it was argued, precluded Congress from taxing the interest on municipal bonds.

In 1988, however, *South Carolina v. Baker*, 485 U.S. 505, made it clear that this is not true now. Case law since Pollock had overturned that decision. See the last section in this chapter for a more extensive discussion of this issue.

TAXATION RULES

Whether and how municipal bonds are taxed varies depending on whether they are bought in the primary or the secondary market and whether they are bought at par, a premium, or a discount.

Issues in the Primary Market

Entities that satisfy the IRS rules can issue tax-exempt bonds. This means that the interest on these bonds is exempt. *Exempt* in this case means that the interest is not included in the federal taxable income of individuals and corporations. This requires a definition of what *interest* is for tax purposes.

Interest is coupon interest. In addition, interest includes the accretion of an original issue discount (OID). The OID measures the amount below par, or 100, that the bond sells for originally, in the primary market. If the investor buys a zero-coupon bond as a new issue for a price of 60, as might happen with a long-term zero-coupon bond, the OID is 40 points (100 − 60). Each year, the price of the bond will rise as it approaches 100 at maturity. This increase in price resulting solely from the passage of time is the accretion of the OID, and it is considered interest for the purposes of tax law.

The Treasury provides symmetrical tax treatment for new issues. If an investor buys a par bond at issue and holds it to maturity, no taxes will be applied on the coupons. At maturity, the price of the bond is 100, the same price as at purchase, so there is no gain or loss and no capital gains consequences.

If an investor buys an OID, the accretion is interest, and since the bond is tax-exempt, the accretion is not taxed by the federal government, as it would be with an OID on a taxable bond. There is no capital gain on the bond resulting from its OID because the price used to calculate the gain, the tax basis, is adjusted upward as time passes. The tax basis at maturity is 100, the same as the bond price, so there is no gain or loss.

In order for there to be symmetry in taxes, bonds that are sold above par in the new issue market must also not have any tax consequences if they are held to maturity. Bonds sold above par at new issue are original issue premiums (OIP). If a bond is originally sold for a price of 107,

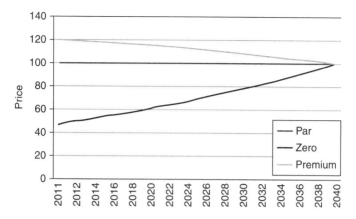

Figure 7-1   Accretion and Amortization, 5 Percent Yield
(*Source:* **Author's calculations.)**

it will be 100 at maturity. If there were no special rule
for OIPs, the bond would have a capital loss of 7 points
(107 − 100) that the bondholder could net against other
capital gains and thus use to save taxes. The IRS requires
the investor to reduce the tax basis of the bond as the bond
price moves toward par. This decline in bond price resulting solely from the passage of time is the amortization of
the bond. Figure 7-1 illustrates the accretion toward par of
a zero-coupon bond and the amortization toward par of a
7 percent coupon premium bond. It also shows that a par
bond with a 5 percent coupon exhibits neither amortization
nor accretion throughout its life.

Discount Bonds in the Secondary Market

There is no tax symmetry for discount bonds in the secondary market. The tax rules that apply in the primary market

for discount bonds do not apply when the bond is purchased in the secondary market.

If a discount bond is bought in the secondary market, it may be a market discount bond. Later we will deal with an exception to this rule, but for now we will assume that a discount bond is a market discount. It is a market discount because interest rates in the market rose after it was issued, making it sell at a discount.

The IRS takes the position that the accretion in the price of a market discount bond is going to happen for certain unless there is a default, and so it is not like a capital gain. With no default, the accretion of a market discount bond is a certainty when a bond is purchased. The rise in price of a discount bond purchased in the secondary market is more like interest. And so the accretion of a market discount bond is taxable income to the investor, and the yearly increase in the price of a market discount bond is taxable income.

The market discount tax rules are some of the most befuddling in the tax code for investors and are very unlikely to give much revenue to the Treasury. That being said, they are an important feature in the pricing of a municipal bond. The basic idea is that in the secondary market, discount bonds are treated differently from the way they are treated in the primary market. The accretion of an OID bond is tax-exempt interest.

The accretion of a bond purchased at a discount in the secondary market may be taxable income. An OID bond can later become a market discount bond, making the accretion on the bond part taxable interest and part tax-exempt interest. Let's take an example. Consider a 30-year-maturity, 5 percent coupon bond issued at par. Suppose that interest rates suddenly rise, driving the price of the bond to 90, and the bond trades to a new buyer. The seller has a tax basis of 100, since the bond was not an OID. When it is sold, the seller experiences a capital loss of 10 points (100 − 90). The buyer has purchased a market discount bond with a tax basis of 90, so the buyer will have to pay tax on the accretion of the bond from 90 to 100.

Any bond can become a market discount bond if interest rates rise after it is issued. If a bond is purchased at a price below its accreted price, or the price that the bond would have at its new-issue yield, it will be a market discount bond. Figure 7-2 shows the accreted price of a zero-coupon, 3 percent coupon, and 4 percent coupon bond, all at a new-issue yield of 5 percent.

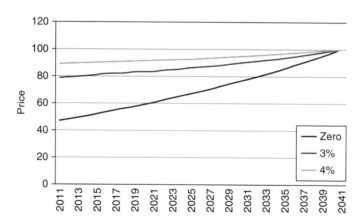

Figure 7-2   OID Accreted Prices, 5 Percent Yield (*Source:* Author's calculations.)

Suppose the 3 percent bond is purchased in 2017 for a price of 70. Originally, the bond had 30 years to maturity (2041 – 2011). But, in the year 2017, the bond will be a 24-year bond (2041 – 2017), and its accreted price will be about 80. This price, 80, is the price that gives a yield of 5 percent. The person who buys the bond may owe ordinary income tax on 10 points (80 – 70) on the market discount bond.

For a par bond, the accreted price is always 100. So, if a 5 percent coupon par bond is purchased in 2017 at a price of 70, the buyer may owe tax on 30 points (100 – 70). Of course, municipal bonds are rarely volatile enough to cause this to happen, and if it were to happen, the seller should probably hold onto the bond and let the bond accrete toward par.

The market discount tax is assumed to be paid upon disposition, that is, call, sink, sale, or maturity. The calculators for discount bonds generally assume that the bond is held to maturity.

The price of the bond adjusts to take into account the tax due. The price of a market discount bond is the price the bond would have without the tax less the present value of the tax.

Let's take an example of a bond issued at par and purchased in the secondary market at a price of 95. This results in a tax on 5 points of discount (100 – 95). If the ordinary income tax rate is 35 percent, the tax due is 1.75 points (0.35×5). The tax is due at maturity, so the price impact declines, as the longer the time until the tax is paid, the smaller is the tax's present value.

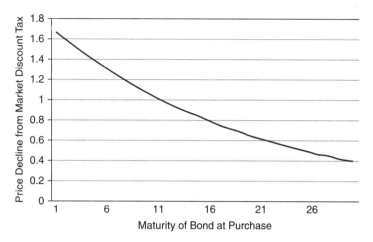

Figure 7-3   Price Impact of 5 Percent Market Discount
(*Source:* Author's calculations.)

Figure 7-3 shows the price impact of the tax, the present value of the tax, as the maturity of the bond varies from 1 to 30 years at a 5 percent discount rate.

Figure 7-3 is an important chart for investors. It shows that the price sensitivity of discount bonds to a specified discount is much higher when the maturity is short. This is exactly the opposite of what is generally assumed about price sensitivity and maturity. Usually, investors believe that the price sensitivity of a bond increases with maturity, but with market discount bonds, that is not necessarily true. Short-maturity discount bonds can have the same price sensitivity as much longer-term par or premium bonds.

Premium Bonds in the Secondary Market

The rules for premium bonds in the secondary market are different from those for discounts. The amortization of the premium is a not a taxable event. Thus, if a bond is purchased at 107 in the secondary market, it will not produce a capital loss as it amortizes to par. The amortization of the premium is not a deduction for tax purposes and does not create a capital loss. Thus, the rules for premium bonds are the same in the primary and secondary markets.

De Minimis

In various places in the federal tax code, Congress has tried to minimize the effect of the code on economic decisions where the amount of tax involved is small. In Latin, "small" is *de minimis*. There are a number of de minimis provisions in the code. Here we will deal with one de minimis rule that focuses on the market discount bond rule.

If the amount of market discount is less than 1/4 point times the number of full years to maturity, then the market discount rule does not apply. In the language of the market, the bond price is "within de minimis."

If a par or premium bond has five years to maturity when it is acquired in the secondary market, then the amount of market discount can be as much as 1.25 points (0.25×5) without triggering the market discount rule. So the price can decline to as much as 98.75 ($100 - 1.25$) without making the accretion of the discount taxable at ordinary income tax rates. If it is more than this amount, the market discount rule applies, but if it is less than this amount, the market discount rule does not apply. If the bond is a par bond, the price can go as low as 98.75 and still be within de minimis. This is also true for OIPs, but the OIP has a bigger cushion because the bond price can fall 1.25 points plus the amount of the premium before the bond becomes a market discount bond.

Of course, the accretion of the discount may still be a taxable event; it is just not ordinary income to the bondholder. Being within de minimis does not mean that the discount is free of taxation; rather, the accretion of the discount is subject to capital gains tax rates, not ordinary income tax rates. Since long-term capital gains rates are typically much lower than ordinary income rates, bonds that are priced within de minimis are less affected by taxes on a discount than bonds that are priced outside of de minimis.

State Taxation

State taxation of interest on municipal bonds varies widely. Most states exempt the interest on in-state bonds for in-state residents. Some, however, do tax the interest on municipal bonds issued within a state and held by state residents. Most states tax the interest on bonds issued by entities outside of the state but held by residents of the state. Capital gains taxes also vary widely; many states tax net capital gains on municipal bonds as ordinary income.

Corporations

Generally, the same tax rules that apply to individuals also apply to corporations. The area is extensive, though, and has many special cases. Here we will consider three general classes of corporate investors: property and casualty insurers (P&Cs), nonfinancial corporations, and financial corporations. Bonds issued in 2009 and 2010 may have different rules applying to them. The discussions provided here do not include the exceptions created by the American Recovery and Reinvestment Act (ARRA) of 2009 as related to some municipal bonds issued in the years 2009 and 2010.

P&Cs

P&Cs are treated differently from other corporations when they hold municipal bonds. They are allowed to carry municipal bonds and to finance their purchases. P&Cs can deduct contributions to their loss reserves. Holding municipal bonds, however, creates a disallowance of part of this deduction. The disallowance equals 15 cents for every dollar of tax-exempt interest earned. This is referred to as *proration*, and it creates an effective tax of 5.25 percent on municipal bond interest when the income tax rate is 35 percent.

Nonfinancials

Most corporations and all individuals are subject to limitations on the ability to deduct interest on borrowings used to buy debt on which the interest is tax-exempt. For individuals, there is no deduction allowed on debt intended to be used to buy tax-exempt securities. Banks and securities firms have their own specialized rules and will be treated separately here.

Nonfinancial corporations can hold tax-exempt securities and deduct the interest on their taxable borrowings as long as the borrowings cannot be traced to the purchase of the tax-exempt securities. Where the debt can be traced to the purchase of the tax-exempt bond, the interest deduction on the debt is not allowed.

Because this type of tracing could easily be very burdensome for a corporation, the IRS provides a safe harbor, a corporate de minimis rule. If the corporation's total holdings of tax-exempts do not exceed 2 percent of its total assets, the corporation is safe from the tracing rule. Given the size of the Fortune 500 firms, these firms could in theory hold vast amounts of municipal bonds and arbitrage the tax-exempt and taxable markets. However, the evidence suggests that this does not occur. Long-term bonds are not a typical investment for a nonfinancial corporation, and the benefits of tax-exempt interest are probably not worth the accounting problems should the IRS do an audit.

Banks and Securities Firms: General Rules

For financial institutions like banks and securities firms, different rules apply. In this case, interest-expense deductions are allowed on a "pro rata" basis. The ratio of the accounting value (adjusted basis) of tax-exempts to the accounting value of total assets times the total interest deduction is used to determine the amount of interest expense that is not allowed (disallowed) as a result of holding tax-exempt bonds.

Bank Small Issue Exemption

The pro rata disallowance of the interest deduction is waived for banks under some circumstances. Where the bank buys a tax-exempt obligation that is a "qualified small issue," it can still deduct a portion of the interest used to carry the issue. The small-issue bonds cannot be private-activity bonds but can be sold by a charitable institution. The bond must be designated as a qualified small issue by the issuer and generally cannot exceed $10 million per year. These bonds trade in the "bank qualified market" or "BQ market" and typically have higher prices than other comparable bonds, reflecting their favorable tax treatment.

The Alternative Minimum Tax

There are two tax systems in the United States: the regular tax and the alternative minimum tax (AMT). The regular tax system is the one that is most familiar to Americans. In the regular tax system, the regular tax rate is applied to the regular taxable income to compute the tax due.

The AMT calculations apply an AMT tax rate to an alternative minimum taxable income (AMTI). This multiplication results in the AMT due. The taxpayer pays the greater of the regular tax or the AMT. The AMT applies to individuals and, with some differences, to corporations. Non-AMT municipal bonds do not have their interest taxed even if the individual is paying the AMT.

For individuals, the calculation of the AMTI begins with the regular taxable income, which is increased by the elimination of exemptions and deductions. Finally, preference items, including the interest on private-purpose municipal bonds, are added into the AMTI, and it is adjusted by an exemption amount. The AMT tax rate is graduated. The rate is 26 percent on AMTI of up to $175,000 in AMTI and 28 percent on AMTI over that for married couples filing jointly. The tax comes into play especially in high-tax states, since state tax deductions are disallowed in calculating the

AMT. The effect for individuals is that the interest on private-purpose municipal bonds is taxable at a marginal rate of 28 percent for high-income individuals who are paying the AMT.

Ten states also have their own AMT codes: California, Colorado, Connecticut, Iowa, Maine, Minnesota, Nebraska, New York, West Virginia, and Wisconsin. State taxes are idiosyncratic, and each is unique; however, the state AMT is computed by multiplying a fixed state alternative minimum tax rate by the taxpayer's state AMTI. The state AMTI is calculated by modifying the individual taxpayer's adjusted gross income by preference items, AMT itemized deductions, and an AMT exemption amount.

Corporate AMT

Corporations face a different AMT. The corporate AMT rate is 20 percent and is applied to the corporate AMTI. Like the individual AMT, the corporate AMTI is increased by preference items, and interest on private-purpose municipal bonds is such a preference item.

The corporate AMT, however, has many unique features, particularly the adjusted current earnings (ACE). The ACE includes all the interest on tax-exempt bonds that has not already been taken into account as a preference item. The corporate AMTI includes 75 percent of the ACE, so under the corporate AMT, private-purpose income is taxed at 20 percent and the rest of a corporation's tax-exempt income is taxed at 15 percent (0.75×20 percent).

Corporations, like individuals, must pay the greater of the regular tax and the AMT. It is important to note, though, that for corporations, the amount of AMT paid above the regular tax is a credit against regular taxes due in future years.

ELIMINATING TAX-EXEMPT MUNICIPALS: CAN THEY? SHOULD THEY?

The budget negotiations going on now in Washington are merely the first round in a protracted effort to find a better balance between the federal government's revenues and expenditures. There seems little doubt that annual deficits on the order of a trillion dollars are untenable if the U.S. dollar is to maintain its reserve currency status.

One seemingly ever-present element in the negotiations is the proposal to eliminate the tax-exempt status of municipal bonds. Given the critical role that tax-exempt bonds have played in the creation of the nation's infrastructure, the hostility of the Treasury Department and some members of Congress to tax-exempt municipal bonds is surprising.

The argument for eliminating tax-exempt bonds has many elements. Here we will provide a brief examination of one of them: are municipals really a tax expenditure?

Constitutional Constraints on Congress

Intergovernmental relations between the federal government and the states have a long and testy history. In *South Carolina v. Baker*, 485 U.S. 505 (1988), the U.S. Supreme Court laid to rest the idea that there was a constitutional protection against the federal government's taxing the interest on state and local bonds. In that case, Congress sought to prohibit the issuance of unregistered bonds in order to reduce tax evasion. The statute applied to private corporations, and indeed the U.S. government, as well as the states. As a result, it was nondiscriminatory.

Congress has made the interest on state and local bonds exempt from federal taxation since the first federal income tax code in 1913. Early interpretations of the intergovernmental tax immunity doctrine, the idea that governments cannot tax one another, supported the exemption. The Court itself held in *Pollock v. Farmers' Loan & Trust Co.*, 157 U.S. 429 (1895), that the interest received on state and local bonds, whether registered or not, was exempt as a result of constitutional law.

In *South Carolina v. Baker*, however, the Court made it clear that the earlier case had been overturned by subsequent law. The Court said, "The owners of state bonds have no constitutional entitlement not to pay taxes on income they earn from the bonds, and States have no constitutional entitlement to issue bonds paying lower interest rates than other issuers."

However, state and local governments are hardly powerless with regard to whether or not their bonds are taxed by the federal government. The Court also said, "Limits on Congress' authority to regulate state activities are structural, not substantive—that is, the States must find their protection from Congressional regulation through the national political process, not through judicially defined spheres of unregulable state activity." The Court is telling the states to confront Congress on matters of tax exemption and not to appeal to the protection of the courts.

Tax Expenditures on Muni Bonds

The idea that tax-exempt interest on municipal bonds is a tax expenditure is an argument that participants in the municipal bond market have heard for many years. Yet, few are familiar with its limitations.

The developer of the "tax expenditure" argument in the United States was Assistant Secretary of the Treasury (Tax Policy) Stanley Surrey. In 1967, in an attempt to motivate Congress to broaden the tax base, he created a list of preferences that Congress had enacted into the tax code. He was spectacularly successful in selling his ideas about tax expenditures. Indeed, tax expenditures are part of the federal budget. Now, as a result of federal law, tax expenditures are defined as: "Revenue losses attributable to provisions of Federal tax laws that allow a special exclusion, exemption, or deduction from gross income or that provide a special credit, a preferential rate of tax, or a deferral of tax liability."

Unfortunately, this hardly qualifies as an accounting definition; rather, it is an invitation for more committee work. With all due respect to the legions of tax lawyers and accountants who have tried to make sense of this definition, it is inherently arbitrary. Consider the current joint committee's methodology:

The normal structure of the individual income tax includes the following major components: one personal exemption for each taxpayer and one for each dependent, the standard deduction, the existing tax rate schedule, and deductions for investment and employee business expenses. Most other tax benefits to individual taxpayers are classified as exceptions to normal income tax law.

Utilizing these definitions has given rise to such clarifying concepts as the "negative" tax expenditure.

For our purposes, the beginning premise is clearly that taxpayer income, without regard to its source, belongs first to the federal government. This is overbroad. Congress has not invidiously discriminated in favor of the states. The states are not a special-interest group seeking preferential treatment but a part of a larger governmental structure with its own tax system.

Expenditure to Whom?

Municipal bonds, in the main, have served to finance public infrastructure and education. Taxing state and local bonds imposes costs for federal programs on much narrower state and local purposes. In this intergovernmental feud, individuals are mere transfer mechanisms, since it is after-tax returns that lie at the core of investor motivations. The externalities associated with federal taxation of municipal bonds may well have the unintended consequences of transferring unrelated federal costs to inherently local needs such as roads and education.

The Court's language in *South Carolina v. Baker* can again be valuable in advising Congress. Treasury instruments are tax-exempt at the state and local level, but that too is not constitutionally protected, and the federal tax exemption is a state tax expenditure:

In sum, then, under current intergovernmental tax immunity doctrine, the States can never tax the United States directly, but can tax any private parties with whom it does business, even though the financial burden falls on the United States, as long as the tax does not discriminate against the United States or those with whom it deals.

What is good for the goose is good for the gander. If the Treasury decides to tax municipal bonds, the taxes paid by investors in state and local debt will come from the issuers. The state and local governments should then look to recoup them through new state taxes on Treasury bonds. Since the state exemption of taxes on federal debt is not constitutionally protected, Congress can appeal only to the state legislatures, not the federal courts.

8

Taxable Municipal Bonds

The previous chapter dealt with tax-exempt municipal bonds, that is, bonds whose interest is not taxed by the federal government. Because the interest rate on tax-exempt bonds has historically been in the range of 80–90 percent of Treasury yields, issuers have aggressively sought to issue bonds on a tax-exempt basis.

However, issuing bonds on a tax-exempt basis is also tightly constrained by the IRS. Governmental-purpose bonds and qualified private-purpose bonds could be sold as tax-exempt bonds. Bonds that did not meet the IRS restrictions, however, had to be sold as taxable bonds. This included pension bonds, whose proceeds were used to acquire assets for public pension funds, and many other bonds. It is important to remember that even though these bonds are federally taxable, they are often exempt from state taxes.

The historical aversion of state and local issuers to selling taxable debt changed, though, with the Build America

Bonds (BABs). BABs were part of an effort to broaden the demand for municipal bonds during the Great Recession. It was also part of an ongoing effort by the Treasury to establish a market for tax-credit bonds. In that respect, the BABs program was at best a limited success.

BABs RULES

BABs issues were allowed to be sold during 2009 and 2010. The BABs program was generally limited to governmental-purpose issues, which could alternatively have been sold as tax-exempt bonds. Private-activity bonds were specifically disallowed. As a result, BABs offered some of the better credits in the market.

The BABs program envisioned two types of bonds: tax-credit and direct-pay. With tax-credit BABs, the bondholder acquired a bond that paid a 35 percent tax credit to the holder rather than a dollar coupon. The credit could be used to pay federal taxes. In addition, the credit could be carried forward or stripped and sold separately. In this way, the Treasury was making a vigorous effort to attract buyers to the program. It was to no avail, though. Investors were leery of future Congresses reducing the subsidy rate and showed little or no interest in the tax-credit program.

If the tax-credit BABs were a failure, the direct-pay BABs were a runaway success. They were a favorite of both issuers and investors during the life of the program. In a direct-pay BAB, the 35 percent subsidy was given to the issuer and not the bondholder, so that the issuer of a BAB got a direct Treasury payment of 35 percent of the coupon

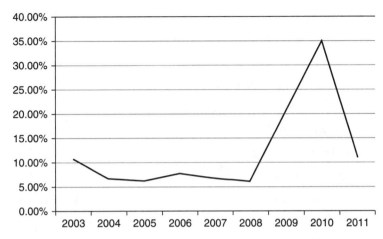

Figure 8-1   Percent of Taxable New Issues, Including BABs (*Source: The Bond Buyer.*)

and sold bonds that were taxable to the buyer. The bond-holder was liable for federal income tax on the BABs, just as with any other taxable bond. At the state level, the interest was typically treated as though the bond were a governmental issue and accordingly was often tax-exempt at the state level. Figure 8-1 offers a picture of the attractiveness of BABs to issuers.

BABs quickly spiked to a significant portion of the market, pushing the total issuance to record heights. In 2009, $64 billion of BABs were sold, and in 2010, $117 billion were issued. The program, however, was not renewed, and issuance quickly fell to zero.

Because longer-term tax-exempt yields rose with the maturity of the bonds, the BAB subsidy was largest for the longest-term bonds. After the issuer included the federal subsidy, the yield it paid on long-term taxable bonds was often on the order of a percentage point lower than it would have paid if it had sold tax-exempt bonds.

The Treasury had initially believed that BABs would be purchased by high-income individuals in lieu of tax-exempt bonds. The program was expected to be very close to tax-neutral, with the investor paying 35 percent of the coupons to the Treasury in taxes, which the Treasury would, in turn, give to the issuer.

Of course, few individuals were so cooperative; individuals primarily bought BABs for tax-sheltered programs like 401(k)s. Moreover, instead of being a retail market, most BABs were purchased by low-taxed or untaxed institutions. The net cost to the federal government grew as BABs issuance surged, and to date, Congress has not extended the program.

Table 8-1 further shows how BABs distorted issuance patterns in the municipal bond sector.

Taxable municipal bond issuance in 2007 was $29.4 billion out of a total of $429.9 billion, or about 7 percent of the market. In 2008, the percentage was a little higher, 11 percent, but still a normal percentage for the market. The

Table 8-1   Taxable Municipal Bond Issuance

Issuance (billions of dollars)	2007	2008	2009	2010
All municipals	429.9	389.6	409.7	433.0
All taxable municipals	29.4	44.6	84.7	151.9
BABs	0	0	64.2	117.3
Other stimulus	0.1	0	3.4	16.8
Other taxable municipals	29.3	44.6	17.1	17.8

Source: The Bond Buyer.

percentage varies from year to year in part because of the periodic sale of large pension-fund bonds.

However, the introduction of BABs in 2009 led taxable issuance to jump to 21 percent of the total in 2009 and 35 percent in 2010. BABs replaced other taxable issuance in 2009 and 2010, pushing those totals down to around 4 percent of the market. At the same time, the rush to sell BABs before their expiration in December 2010 moved a large amount of 2011 issuance into 2010. BABs issuance as well as budgetary problems in state and local governments led to a 50 percent decline in total issuance in the first part of 2011.

OTHER STIMULUS BONDS

In addition to BABs, Congress has also created several other classes of tax-credit bonds, including:

- Clean renewable energy bonds (CREBs)
- Qualified energy conservation bonds (QECBs)
- Qualified zone academy bonds (QZABs)
- Qualified school construction bonds (QSCBs)
- Recovery zone economic development bonds (RZEDBs)

Each of these programs has a unique set of rules and is much less common than BABs. These issues have had only modest success in the market, again because of the limited demand for tax-credit bonds, and also because of the small amounts authorized for these programs. They can be surprisingly complex. The Treasury directly sets the subsidy rates for some of these bonds.

A BAB EXAMPLE

Here we examine some of the features of a BAB. This example also provides an opportunity to compare tax-exempt and taxable bond structures as well as the differences in taxation. We will look at several important features of the City of San Antonio Electric and Gas Systems Revenue Bonds.

A portion of the cover of the OS is reproduced in Figure 8-2.

Unlike with tax-exempt bonds, there are no serial bonds. The issue follows the corporate bond style of having a single bond with a face value equal to the total par value of the issue, $375,000,000. The dated date is the date the deal closes and the underwriter pays for the bonds.

This is a direct subsidy Build America Bond, so the issuer is going to get a payment from the U.S. Treasury of

MATURITIES, INTEREST RATES AND PRICING SCHEDULE

$375,000,000

CITY OF SAN ANTONIO, TEXAS

ELECTRIC AND GAS SYSTEMS REVENUE BONDS,

TAXABLE NEW SERIES 2009C

(DIRECT SUBSIDY - BUILD AMERICA BONDS)

Dated May 1, 2009 (Interest to accrue from Closing on June 12, 2009)

Stated Maturity	Principal Amount	Interest Rate (percent)	Initial Yield (percent)	CUSIP
1-Feb-39	$375,000,000	5.985	5.985	

Figure 8-2   Title

Figure 8-3   Interest Not Exempt

35 percent of the interest on the bond. The coupon on the bond, 5.985 percent, is also corporate style and was probably the result of an option-pricing model, which we will discuss later.

The title page of the OS declares that the bonds are taxable (see Figure 8-3). The interest is federally taxable, since the income is not *excluded from* gross income. Compare this with the tax-exempt bonds, where the interest is not *included in* gross income.

The bonds are being used for capital improvements to the electrical system and are to be repaid from the net revenues of the system (see Figure 8-4).

This bond, like the tax-exempt term bonds we have seen, has mandatory sinking fund redemption in the last years of the life of the bond (see Figure 8-5).

And like tax-exempt issues of the city, these bonds are not subject to SEC disclosure rules and are not SEC registered. The fact that the bonds are taxable does not make a state or local issue subject to SEC supervision. However, of

The Bonds are being issued to: (i) finance costs associated with constructing capital improvements of the Systems and (ii) pay costs and expenses relating to their issuance. The Bonds are payable from and equally and ratably secured, together with the currently outstanding Senior Lien Obligations, solely by a first and prior lien on and pledge of the Net Revenues (defined herein) of the Systems.

Figure 8-4   Purpose

Mandatory Redemption of Bonds

The Bonds maturing on February 1, 2039 (the "Term Bonds") are subject to mandatory redemption prior to maturity in part by lot, at a price equal to the principal amount thereof plus accrued interest to the date of redemption, on February 1 in the respective years and principal amounts shown below:

Redemption Date	Redemption Amount
February 1, 2033	$23,151,000
February 1, 2034	24,054,000
February 1, 2035	60,653,000
February 1, 2036	63,012,000
February 1, 2037	65,464,000
February 1, 2038	68,010,000
February 1, 2039	70,656,000

Figure 8-5   Redemption

course, the antifraud provisions of the federal securities laws do apply, as Figure 8-6 declares.

The optional redemption on this bond is different from those usually found in a tax-exempt issue. Here the optional redemption is not a pure interest-rate call. There is no call protection; the call can occur at any time after issuance.

Here the call is a *make-whole redemption*. The language is a little complex (see Figure 8-7), but essentially the call price is the greater of par or a premium. The amount of the

THE BONDS ARE EXEMPT FROM REGISTRATION WITH THE UNITED STATES SECURITIES AND EXCHANGE COMMISSION AND CONSEQUENTLY HAVE NOT BEEN REGISTERED THEREWITH. THE REGISTRATION, QUALIFICATION, OR EXEMPTION OF THE BONDS IN ACCORDANCE WITH APPLICABLE SECURITIES LAW PROVISIONS OF THE JURISDICTIONS IN WHICH THESE BONDS HAVE BEEN REGISTERED, QUALIFIED, OR EXEMPTED SHOULD NOT BE REGARDED AS A RECOMMENDATION FOR THE PURCHASE THEREOF.

NEITHER THE UNITED STATES SECURITIES AND EXCHANGE COMMISSION NOR ANY STATE SECURITIES COMMISSION HAS APPROVED OR DISAPPROVED OF THE BONDS OR PASSED UPON THE ADEQUACY OR ACCURACY OF THIS DOCUMENT. ANY REPRESENTATION TO THE CONTRARY IS A CRIMINAL OFFENSE.

Figure 8-6   SEC Notice

Redemption of Bonds

Optional Redemption. The Bonds are subject to redemption on any date, at the City's option at a redemption price equal to the Make-Whole Redemption Price. The Bonds are redeemable, in whole or in part, and if in part, by lot or other customary method within such maturity.

The "Make-Whole Redemption Price" is equal to the greater of (i) the issue price of the Bonds set forth on the inside cover page hereof (but not less than 100%) of the principal amount of the Bonds to be redeemed or (ii) the sum of the present value of the remaining scheduled payments of principal of and interest on the Bonds to be redeemed to the maturity date of such Bonds . . . discounted to the date on which the Bonds are to be redeemed on a semi-annual basis, assuming a 360-day year containing twelve 30-day months, at the Treasury Rate (defined below) plus twenty-five (25) basis points, plus accrued interest on the Bonds to be redeemed to the redemption date.

Figure 8-7   Make-Whole Provision

premium is determined by discounting the bond cash flow at the Treasury yield plus 25 basis points (0.25 percent). This approach can give the bondholder a premium call price. For the issuer, it is an alternative to a tender or an offer to buy the bonds in the secondary market.

The city is also protecting itself from future congressional capriciousness. If the 35 percent subsidy is reduced or eliminated, and this is not an impossible proposition, the action may result in these bonds being called (see Figure 8-8). Concern about future Congresses changing tax law to the disadvantage of bondholders is also one of the central concerns in tax-subsidy bonds.

Extraordinary Redemption

Because the Bonds are issued as Build America bonds, the Bonds will be subject to extraordinary optional redemption prior to their stated maturities, at the option of the City . . . if the City determines that a material adverse change has occurred . . . pursuant to which the Tax Credit is reduced or eliminated.

Figure 8-8   Tax-Credit Call

The City has covenanted . . . that it will at all times maintain rates and charges for the sale of electric energy, gas, or other services . . . reasonably expected to produce gross revenues sufficient to pay all maintenance and operating expenses of the Systems, and to produce Net Revenues sufficient, together with other lawfully available funds, to pay debt service requirements on all revenue debt of the Systems.

Figure 8-9   Rate Covenant

Figure 8-9 shows that the city gives the bondholder a rate covenant, or agreement, that binds it to set electrical and other rates high enough to meet the debt service on the bonds.

Finally, Figure 8-10 shows that the state law remedy for default is spelled out as a writ of mandamus.

Registered Owners' Remedies

If the City defaults in the payment of principal, interest, or redemption price on the Bonds when due, or if it fails to make payments into any fund or funds created in the Ordinance, or defaults in the observation or performance of any other covenants, conditions, or obligations set forth in the Ordinance, the registered owners may seek a writ of mandamus to compel City officials to carry out their legally imposed duties with respect to the Bonds.

Figure 8-10   Mandamus Remedy Required

9

The Microstructure of the Municipal Bond Market

Here we will give a broad overview of the municipal bond market. We will look at the market from 30,000 feet and see the size of the market, both in absolute numbers and relative to the taxable market and the economy as a whole. The types of bonds issued and who buys them will be central themes. After that, we will examine the market by state, showing which states have the most debt outstanding by type. The chapter focuses on fixed-coupon issuance, but at the end of this chapter, one of the most important types of variable-rate bonds, variable-rate demand obligations (VRDOs), is discussed.

More Market Shorthand

VRDO   Variable Rate Demand Obligation

Long-term bonds that trade as short-term instruments because of liquidity guarantee of two types:

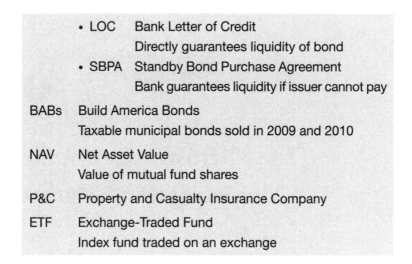

- LOC   Bank Letter of Credit
          Directly guarantees liquidity of bond
- SBPA   Standby Bond Purchase Agreement
          Bank guarantees liquidity if issuer cannot pay

BABs   Build America Bonds
        Taxable municipal bonds sold in 2009 and 2010

NAV   Net Asset Value
        Value of mutual fund shares

P&C   Property and Casualty Insurance Company

ETF   Exchange-Traded Fund
        Index fund traded on an exchange

THE PRIMARY MARKET

The volume of newly issued municipal bonds rose to a record of $434 billion in 2010, as Figure 9-1 shows. The surge was due primarily to a Build America Bonds (BABs) rush to

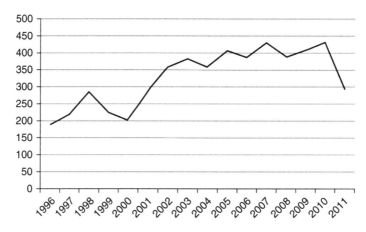

Figure 9-1   Annual Municipal Bond Issuance (billions of dollars) (*Source:* SIFMA.)

market, as Congress let the very popular subsidy bond program lapse in 2011.

As we can see in the figure, municipal bond issuance has been trending upward for many years. Several factors are responsible for the increase. First, the issuance is in nominal dollars, and inflation will force the issuance of larger amounts to support the same level of infrastructure financing. Rising population is another consideration, as is increasing per-capita wealth. Larger and wealthier populations demand and can afford to pay for bigger and better public-sector facilities.

The increase in volume, however, is not a reflection of reckless borrowing. Taken as a whole, state and local governments have been conservative in their debt management, which has been one important reason for the low default rates on municipal bonds. States have been especially careful in borrowing with general obligation bonds (GOs). For example, the issuance of a GO usually requires an election in which the majority of the voters need to authorize the sale of the bonds.

The states did not participate in the financial leveraging of the U.S. economy in the 2000s. Figure 9-2 shows that back around the year 2000, municipal bond issuance was about 60 percent of Treasury issuance. Now the ratio is closer to 10 percent.

Figure 9-3 shows the relative amounts of municipal bonds and corporate bonds outstanding since the 1980s. The municipal and corporate bond markets were roughly the same size in the early 1980s. Since then, the ratio of outstanding municipal to outstanding corporate bonds has been on an irregular trend downward, until the municipal bond

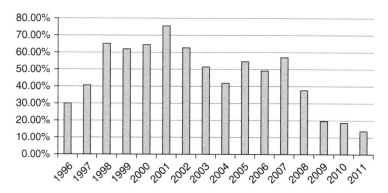

Figure 9-2   Municipal Bond Issuance as a Percentage of Treasury Issuance (*Source:* SIFMA.)

market is now half that of corporates. The municipal bond market has also shrunk relative to the whole U.S. fixed-income market, as Figure 9-3 also displays.

Further evidence that the muni market has not been a source of leverage in the overall economy comes from comparing the stock of outstanding municipal bonds to the overall size of the U.S. economy. The stock of municipal bonds in

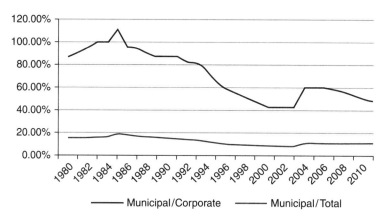

Figure 9-3   Relative Amounts of Municipal Bonds Outstanding Since the 1980s (*Source:* SIFMA.)

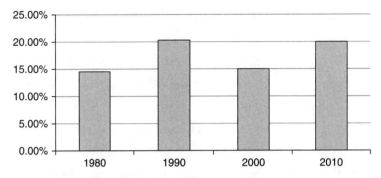

Figure 9-4   Municipal Bonds Outstanding Relative to Nominal U.S. GDP (*Source:* SIFMA and U.S. Census Bureau.)

the market has remained in the 15 to 20 percent range of the overall economy for many years. In fact, Figure 9-4 shows that the outstanding stock of municipals is no higher as a proportion of the economy than it was in 1990. This indicates that the states did not try to borrow their way out of the Great Recession.

Even though the ratio in Figure 9-4 has been relatively steady, it is not without controversy. Whether this municipal debt should be added to the Treasury debt in determining the ratio of debt to GDP to make U.S. debt ratios more comparable to those of other countries with less developed municipal markets has been a continuing concern. In large part, whether to add municipal debt to Treasury debt depends on the status of the states. The states are sovereigns in their own right. Clearly the rating agencies see them as being independent of the central government. Indeed, Moody's has indicated that several states, but hardly all, may risk downgrades because of an excessive dependence on the Treasury for finances.

Even if one views the states as U.S. subsovereigns for this purpose, it would be appropriate to include only the GOs and to exclude the self-sustaining revenue debt. Revenue debt is self-sustaining because the debt service is to be repaid from project revenues and not general tax revenues.

At the end of 2010, SIFMA data showed that only 20 percent of the outstanding municipal bonds were GOs. Including these would increase the Treasury debt ratio by about 4 percentage points and make little material difference in the international debt-to-GDP discussions.

Maturity Profile

The dominant use of revenue bonds to finance long-dated infrastructure like roads and buildings means that municipal bonds tend to have long maturities. Historically, as Figure 9-5 shows, the average maturity of a municipal bond has been in the 16- to 21-year range.

Municipal bonds are also significantly longer in maturity than corporate bonds. This is shown in Figure 9-6, where

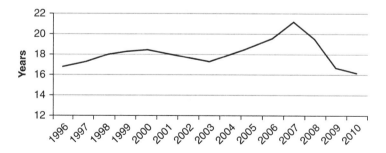

Figure 9-5   Average Maturity of Municipal Bonds Issued, by Year (*Source:* SIFMA.)

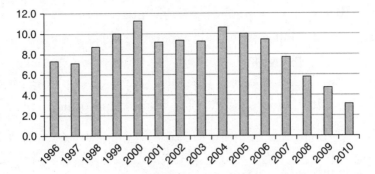

Figure 9-6   Municipal Bond Maturity Minus Corporate Bond Maturity, by Year (*Source:* SIFMA.)

we can see that municipals have historically been about 8 to 10 years longer than corporate bonds.

Recently the difference has fallen, as corporations have been selling more long-term debt to avoid liquidity problems from having to roll over short-term financings, as well as to take advantage of very low long-term rates.

Issuance by Purpose

The use of proceeds for a bond issue identifies the purpose for which the borrowing is used. These bond purposes parallel the investment profile of state and local governments. The standard classifications are provided by *The Bond Buyer* newspaper. *The Bond Buyer*'s sectors include:

- Development: construction of nongovernmental buildings, such as offices
- Education: investment in all levels of public education
- Environmental facilities: recycling, solid waste, and pollution control investments

- Electric power: public power facilities
- General purpose: a wide range of public-sector investments, including agriculture and other public buildings
- Healthcare: a broad category that includes hospitals, hospital equipment, nursing homes, and other medical facilities
- Housing: a category that includes single-family and multifamily housing
- Public facilities: a wide spectrum of parks, police stations, fire stations, libraries, and museums
- Transportation: highways, airports, seaports, mass transit, toll roads, and others
- Utilities: water and sewer, gas, telecommunications, flood control, sanitation, and others

Figure 9-7 shows the amount outstanding by use of proceeds at the end of 2010. Education was the largest use of proceeds for which municipal bonds were issued. Among

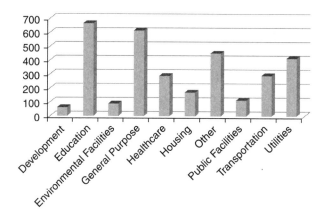

Figure 9-7   Municipal Bonds Outstanding by Type, 2010 (billions of dollars) (*Source:* SIFMA.)

the specifically identified categories, transportation and utilities were important uses, as were healthcare and housing. As one would expect, the "general purpose" and "other" categories were large catchall groups.

In a typical year, more GOs than revenue bonds are sold, but the revenue issues are larger. In 2010, for example, there were 8,423 issues of GOs, raising $147.7 billion. The average size of a GO issue was only $17.5 million. Nevertheless, 83 percent of these issues were rated, which is consistent with the high quality of the sector. Most of the GO issuance, $78 billion, was devoted to general purposes, since bonds backed by the taxing power of the issuer should have wide social benefits. The next-largest use of GO debt was for education, $48 billion.

Revenue bonds were sold for a variety of purposes in 2010. Overall, however, fewer revenue bonds were sold than GOs, but because of their larger size, the revenue sector was more than twice as large as the GO-backed bonds. In total, 5,466 revenue bond issues were sold in 2010, raising $285.3 billion. This gives an average issue size of $52.2 million for revenue bonds. Only 728 issues were not rated, and only 9 issues were rated below investment grade, showing that revenue bonds too are typically a high-grade sector.

Transportation leads the list of use of proceeds for revenue bonds at $57 billion, followed closely by education at $51 billion. For the year, the combined GO and revenue borrowings for education totaled almost $100 billion in a single year, which clearly shows the continuing commitment of state and local governments to education.

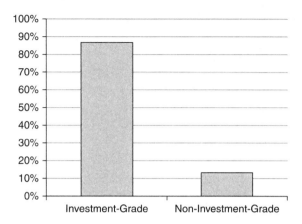

**Figure 9-8   Percentage of Bonds Outstanding by Rating, 2010
(*Source:* SIFMA.)**

Many investors are looking for higher-yielding, lower-rated municipal bonds. The issuance of high-yield municipal bonds varies some by year as well, but it is generally small. Figure 9-8 shows that overall, only about 13 percent of the outstanding issues in 2010 were non-investment-grade. The "junk" category for municipal bonds is a relatively small and specialized segment of the market.

Outstanding by State

All the states have municipal bonds outstanding. In 2010, California had the largest amount of total debt outstanding (see Figure 9-9). The state had $483 billion, of which $110 billion were GOs. New York was next at $339 billion; of those, $61 billion were GOs. Even if a state had a fairly large total amount outstanding, the GO portion could be very small. For example, Florida had $170 billion in total

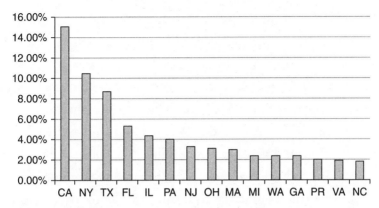

**Figure 9-9   Percentage of Bonds Outstanding by State, 2010
(*Source:* SIFMA.)**

outstanding municipal bonds, of which only $7 billion was general obligation. This is important because the revenue debt is generally self-supporting, whereas the taxing power of the state or its political subdivisions is exposed for the GOs.

The vast majority of the debt was long-term and not notes. In the municipal bond market, notes are securities that mature in 13 months or less. About 5 percent of the municipal debt outstanding was notes, and the rest was longer-term bonds. Taken as a whole, state and local governments have very little rollover risk or the need to sell new short-term borrowings as old ones mature. The largest amounts of short-term debt are concentrated in a few states. California has $29 billion in notes, New York $18 billion, and Texas $16 billion. Compared to the size of their economies, even these are small amounts.

More than a trillion of the total debt outstanding in the municipal bond market remains insured, mostly as a result of prior insurance contracts. The demise of the credit ratings of the majority of the companies in the municipal bond insurance industry did not necessarily affect a bond's insured status. If a bond was insured, it remained insured, without regard to the quality of the insurer. For the most part, though, the bond insurance of the low-rated insurers has little, if any, value. In fact, depending upon the status of the insurer, the bond may even be penalized in price as a result of continuing to have insurance. And because of the high credit quality of the insurers at the time the bonds were issued, many insured bonds may not have ratings on the underlying bond, severely limiting their liquidity.

THE SECONDARY MARKET

The secondary market for municipal bonds is an active over-the-counter (OTC) market. However, its liquidity has declined in recent years with the loss of several large dealers and many arbitrage accounts. In 2006 and 2007, trading volume was typically on the order of $25 billion per day. By 2010, it had declined to $15 billion per day. More recently, EMMA trading volume has fallen to about $10 billion per day.

The number of trades, however, has increased from the mid–thirty thousands per day to more than forty thousand a day. The average trade is now around $250,000. The decline in average trade size and the increase in the number of trades reflect the rising demand for liquidity from retail investors. Figure 9-10 shows that for 2010, 82 percent of all trades were less than $100,000 in par value.

Trading has remained concentrated in a few dealer firms. The top five dealers accounted for 43.9 percent of all

Less than $100,000	*82%*
$100,001–$500,000	*12%*
$500,001–$1,000,000	*2%*
$1,000,000+	*4%*

**Figure 9-10   Percentage of Trades by Trade Size, 2010
(*Source:* SIFMA.)**

customers trading. And trading is concentrated in the most recently issued bonds. The vast majority of trading in a bond occurs within the first three months after the bond was issued. After that, the likelihood that a bond will be traded falls off rapidly. By the time a bond has been outstanding for several years, its trading activity is very low. Part of the reason for this is that many bonds are "put away" and held to maturity. In addition, when the issuer has not kept up with regular disclosures, the information cost of buying a seasoned issue can be prohibitively high.

The Holders

The municipal bond market has a diverse set of investors. They range from the well-known, U.S. high-net-worth individual investor group to a growing number of international institutions. The Federal Reserve reports that there are $3.7 trillion in outstanding municipal bonds. Of that, $2.9 trillion are long-term and only $52 billion are short term.

As Figure 9-11 shows, direct holdings by individual investors account for fully half of the investment in municipal bonds.

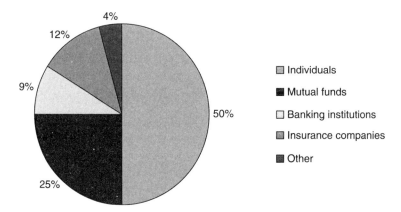

Figure 9-11   Distribution of Municipal Investors, 2011
(*Source:* Federal Reserve.)

The nature of the individual investors in the municipal bond market is often misunderstood. These "high-net-worth" investors are frequently characterized as superrich. Certainly that is true for some, but the IRS data suggest that most municipal bond investors are not materially different from investors in corporate bonds and equities.

In Figure 9-12 we can see the percentage of income received from different types of investments by adjusted gross income (AGI).

It is investors in the $100,000–$200,000 AGI group who receive the highest percentage of taxable interest and tax-exempt interest. A relatively small percentage of tax-exempt income goes to the very wealthiest group. One reason for this may be that retail investors often consider municipal bond investments to be their "safe money." In essence, retail investors view their municipal bond income as their reservation wage. If everything else fails, they will still have their municipal bonds. It is for this reason that many retail investors are

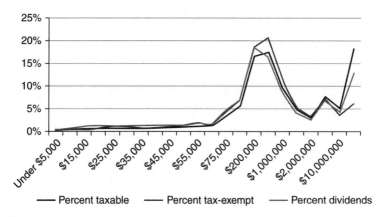

Figure 9-12   Percentage of Individual Investors' Income by AGI (*Source:* Internal Revenue Service.)

very risk-averse or actual risk avoiders. This risk intolerance also explains how insurance became so dominant a force in the municipal bond market. Individual investors are willing to demand insurance on bonds that are already regarded as having some of the lowest risk in the fixed-income markets.

Figure 9-12 also shows that the investors with the very highest AGIs receive the largest percentage of all dividends. This is consistent with the idea that many of these individuals own small companies. In addition, the need for a safe asset declines as the absolute amount of wealth reaches very high levels.

Mutual funds make up the next largest group, as shown in Figure 9-11, at 25 percent. There are three types of mutual funds in the total. Long-term mutual funds have $540 billion in municipal bonds, followed by money market funds, with about $300 billion, and closed-end funds, with about $80 billion. Long-term bond funds and money market funds are open-ended funds that continuously buy and sell their shares. The net asset value (NAV) of the fund is calculated once a day. All the buys and sells for an open-ended fund are done at the NAV.

Closed-end funds, by contrast, sell shares only once, when the fund is formed. The shares trade on an exchange, and investors can buy and sell them for whatever the market demands at the time of the trade. Closed-end funds may also employ leverage, that is, they can borrow funds to buy bonds. All of the mutual funds invest in municipal bonds and pass interest and capital gains from the bonds to the mutual fund investors. Investors receive the same tax treatment on the investment that they would if they owned the bonds directly.

There is a vast array of mutual funds. Many of them are state-specific and buy bonds that are treated favorably by a particular state. As always, however, investors should consult tax professionals about any specific investment.

While still relatively small at $11 billion in outstanding value, exchange-traded funds (ETFs) offer investors yet another alternative investment structure for municipal bonds. As the name implies, an ETF trades on a stock exchange and is continuously priced by the market. ETFs generally are designed to track an index, and so, like closed-end funds, they are a passive form of investment. Open-ended funds, by contrast, are usually actively managed.

Insurance companies include life as well as property and casualty insurance companies (P&Cs). Insurance companies hold about 12 percent of all municipal bonds. Life insurance companies typically are in a lower tax bracket than P&Cs. As a result, life insurance holdings of municipal bonds tend to be taxable municipals, especially Build America Bonds

(BABs). BABs are attractive because of their high credit quality, relative cheapness, and long duration. P&C municipal bond portfolios will tend to hold tax-exempt municipals, reflecting the 35 percent marginal tax bracket for these firms.

Wells Fargo, Wachovia, and Citibank were among the largest bank holders of municipal bonds in 2011. The relative cheapness of tax-exempt municipal bonds has been an important factor attracting bank interest in the municipal market. In addition, special rules temporarily applied to bank purchases of municipal bonds under the American Recovery and Reinvestment Act of 2009 (ARRA) before it ended at the end of 2010. The bill increased the bank eligible size from $10 to $30 million and also granted the banks the 2 percent de minimis exception, which nonfinancial firms employ, for two years.

Foreign institutions, particularly banks, hold about $83 billion in municipal bonds. For these institutions, taxable municipal bonds offer a high-grade sovereign diversification vehicle.

VARIABLE-RATE DEMAND OBLIGATIONS

Variable-rate demand obligations (VRDOs) made up $392 billion of the total outstanding municipal bonds in 2010. VRDOs are long-term bonds that are puttable at par plus accrued interest by the holder. That is, the purchaser of the bond can, at its option, sell the bond back to a remarketing agent, an entity designated by the issuer to make a market in the VRDO. The interest paid on a VRDO varies over time and is typically reset either daily or weekly so that the VRDO trades at par. These instruments are designed to be sold to money market funds or very large investors in denominations of $100,000.

The pricing and placement of VRDOs are managed by investment banks on behalf of the issuer. When the buyer of the VRDO seeks to liquidate its position, it will sell the bond to a bank. Should the remarketing agent at the bank not be able to find another buyer for the VRDO, it can, in turn, put the security back to the trustee or another institution, including the issuer, that the issuer designates.

The ability of the dealer to tender rests on the liquidity support purchased by the issuer. The liquidity support is a contract sold to the issuer, usually by a bank, that guarantees that the VRDOs will be bought for cash on demand. These contracts are of two general types: letters of credit (LOCs) or standby bond purchase agreements (SBPAs).

In a direct LOC, the bank is the first source of liquidity, backed up by the issuer. Indeed, as the letter of credit is direct obligation of the bank, the bank's rating is looked to as the primary credit. Like an LOC, an SBPA provides a liquidity backup. With a standby agreement, the bank selling the agreement will provide the cash to buy the VRDO if the issuer cannot. There are often a great many more conditions applied to an SBPA than there are to the usual letter of credit. For example, the standby agreement's support can be lost if the issuer's rating falls below investment grade or is suspended. In spite of this, the VRDO market is liquid and highly rated. VRDOs are normally given the highest short-term ratings and are eligible for purchase by money market funds. However, the increased cost of the bank liquidity facilities in recent years has been an

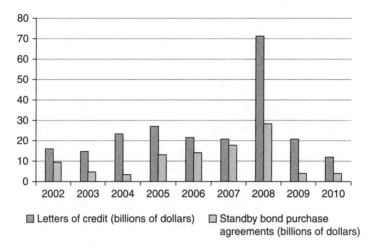

Figure 9-13   Liquidity Support for VRDOs, by Type
(*Source:* SIFMA.)

important reason for the decline in the size of the VRDO market generally.

Liquidity support of all types has declined in recent years, as Figure 9-13 shows. Nevertheless, there are a myriad of VRDO contracts with many variations of liquidity agreements. An investor in a VRDO will need to review the contract in detail to understand the nature of the security.

VRDOs have also faced competition from direct bank purchases of variable-rate debt. For the borrower, this reduces the risk of rolling over short-term LOCs and SBPAs. Banks buying VRDOs are investing in a high-quality floating-rate bond that offers an attractive interest-rate spread.

The SIFMA Municipal Swap Index

VRDO rates are the basis of the SIFMA Municipal Swap Index. The SIFMA Municipal Swap Index was previously

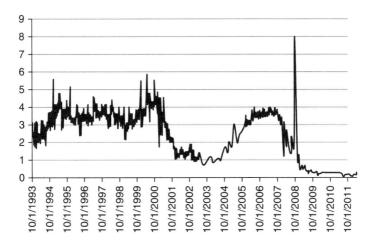

Figure 9-14   SIFMA Municipal Swap Index History
(*Source:* SIFMA.)

known as the Bond Market Association/PSA Municipal Swap Index. It is produced weekly by Municipal Market Data (MMD) and is based on an average of seven-day rates paid the previous week by a large sample of high-quality VRDOs. Among other requirements, the interest on the VRDOs in the sample must be tax-free, and the VRDOs must have at least $10 million in outstanding par amount. Because these instruments qualify for purchase by money market funds, this index is typically a very low money market rate. The history of index rates is shown in Figure 9-14. The extraordinary spike to 8 percent in 2008 is the result of the Lehman bankruptcy.

It is important to distinguish VRDOs from auction-rate securities. Rates on VRDOs are reset weekly based on an index, whereas auction-rate securities, as the name implies, have their rates established by an auction. During the financial crisis of the last decade, the vast majority of these auctions failed, and many continue to fail. In a failed auction, the interest rate on the security changes to the maximum rate established when the bonds were sold.

For most of the failed auctions, the interest rate was reset to a very high number, such as 12 percent or 15 percent. This was designed to force the issuers to refinance the auction-rate securities, and that is indeed what happened in many cases. Other times, either the maximum rate proved to be an extremely low rate or the credit position of the issuer did not allow it to sell new bonds to refinance auction-rate bonds that were priced at their maximum rate. The result is that there are still $64 billion in auction-rate securities outstanding, many of them highly illiquid.

The cost of credit support and reduced demand from money market funds has led to a rapid reduction in the size of the auction-rate market. Concern about the performance of the auction-rate process resulted in the cessation of issuance of these securities. See Figure 9-15.

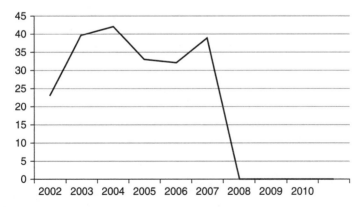

Figure 9-15   Auction-Rate Securities Issuance (*Source: The Bond Buyer.*)

10

State and Local Economies

In order to appreciate the nature of municipal bond credits, it is useful to get a better sense of the economics of state and local governments. In order to do that, we will look briefly at the size of these economies, followed by a review of the sources of state and local government revenue, and then a review of state and local government expenditures.

Knowing where the money comes from tells us how the bonds can be repaid, and knowing what governments do with the money tells us what types of bonds state and local governments issue.

GROSS DOMESTIC PRODUCT (GDP) BY STATE

The U.S. states are massive financial entities. Merely reciting the official statistics on state GDPs (also called the gross state products) does not bring home the real scale of these institutions. Instead, a comparison of states with other countries

161

is more effective. The *Economist* provides a nice summary of where the states' economies stand relative to other countries. The largest U.S. state economy, California, headed the state GDP list in 2009 at $1.9 trillion. This is roughly equivalent to Italy's $2.1 trillion economy. Texas's $1.1 trillion economy is roughly equal to Russia's $1.2 trillion economy. The state of Washington and the country of Greece both had about $300 billion in GDP, although Greece's has been declining recently.

The point here is simply that the range and scale of state activities and their bond markets rival those of many countries. As a result, we would expect the states to be involved in financing a wide range of governmental activities, and we will find that the municipal bond market reflects this complexity.

STATE AND LOCAL REVENUE

The U.S. Census Bureau provides extensive data on state and local government receipts and expenditures. In 2008, state and local governments collected $2.66 trillion. About half of that amount, or $1.6 trillion, went to the states, with the remainder going to local governments. In Figure 10-1, we see that tax revenue accounted for about 50 percent of the total state and local government receipts. The federal government provides 18 percent of the revenue, much of it to fund federally mandated programs that the states administer.

Figure 10-2 examines the types of taxes that states impose. Property taxes and sales taxes each accounted for about one-third of the total. Income taxes were about one-quarter in 2008.

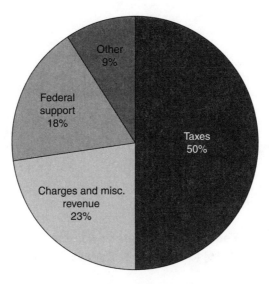

Figure 10-1   Sources of State and Local Government Revenue, 2008 (*Source:* U.S. Census Bureau.)

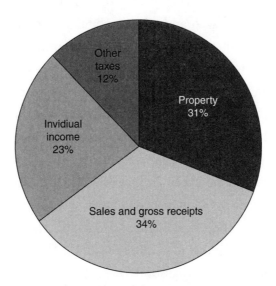

Figure 10-2   State and Local Government Tax Revenue, 2008 (*Source:* U.S. Census Bureau.)

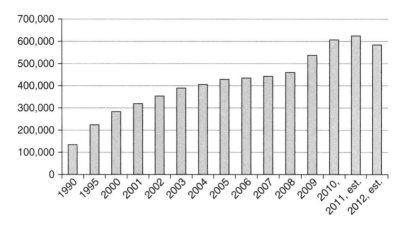

Figure 10-3   Federal Aid to State and Local Governments (millions of dollars) (*Source:* U.S. Census Bureau.)

There is a wide variety of state and local taxes. Sales taxes accounted for about 34 percent, followed by property taxes at 31 percent, individual income taxes at 23 percent, and other taxes at 12 percent. Virtually all of the miscellaneous revenues from alcohol, tobacco, and other such taxes went to the states.

Federal grants to state and local governments have been a growing source of revenue over the years (see Figure 10-3). These grants tend to accelerate during the years following recessions because state and local income lags the economy by several years. The increases in 2009 and 2010 were in line with those in prior recessionary periods. The growth in federal grants can be expected to slow and may even shrink going forward as Congress struggles with containing the federal deficit. Indeed, as Figure 10-3 shows, the U.S. Census Bureau expects grants to decline for 2012. This would be the first year-over-year reduction since 1987.

The information in Table 10-1 is important. Given the federal budget problems, these discretionary programs are

Table 10-1   Program Expenditures, 2012

Program	2012, est.
Total (millions of dollars)	584,278
Energy	2,816
Natural resources and environment	7,765
Environmental Protection Agency	5,289
Agriculture	962
Transportation	70,712
Grants for airports	3,481
Federal-aid highways	43,198
Urban mass transportation	15,383
Community and regional development	14,801
Community development fund	7,807
Homeland Security	3,500
State and local programs	2,339
Disaster relief	1,156
Education, training, employment and social services	70,129
Education for the disadvantaged	16,307
School improvement programs	5,148
Special education	13,877
Social services—block grant	1,802
Children and family services programs	8,969
Training and employment services	3,155
Health	288,826
Substance abuse and mental health services	2,965
Grants to states for Medicaid	269,068
State children's health insurance fund	9,781
Income security	110,863
SNAP (formerly Food Stamp Program)	6,655
Child nutrition programs	18,728
Temporary assistance for needy families	17,205
Veterans' benefits and services	1,011
Administration of justice	5,720

Source: U.S. Census Bureau.

likely to be under great scrutiny. These are also areas where states may well have to increase their expenditures to make up for lost federal transfers.

The dependence of state and local governments on federal grants differs widely. At the local level, only 3.8 percent of revenues came from federal grants in 2008, while at the state level, 26.1 percent of the revenues came from the federal government. Table 10-2 shows the grants by state. California, New York, and Texas dominate the list by a wide margin.

STATE AND LOCAL EXPENDITURES

Figure 10-4 shows the breakdown of combined state and local expenditures. These are the investments in public infrastructure and other public activities that the state and local governments engage in.

State and local expenditures are concentrated in education (29 percent), public welfare (14 percent), trust and pension funds (8 percent), utilities (7 percent), highways (5 percent), and hospitals (5 percent). The many other activities of state and local governments absorb the other 32 percent of expenditures.

Like the revenues, the expenditures vary by level of government. Education (13.4 percent) and aid to the poor (20.4 percent) were the largest expenditures at the state level. At the local level, education was also a major expenditure (37.3 percent), but public welfare was not (3.2 percent). Water, gas, and other utilities were virtually all the domain of local governments.

Table 10-2   Federal Grants by State, 2009 (millions of dollars)

Total	552,108
Alabama	7,610
Alaska	3,624
Arizona	12,997
Arkansas	5,598
California	61,971
Colorado	6,333
Connecticut	6,759
Delaware	1,679
District of Columbia	9,659
Florida	22,686
Georgia	12,953
Hawaii	2,560
Idaho	2,458
Illinois	20,941
Indiana	10,194
Iowa	5,033
Kansas	3,965
Kentucky	8,245
Louisiana	11,534
Maine	3,399
Maryland	9,405
Massachusetts	15,200
Michigan	16,580
Minnesota	9,304
Mississippi	7,642
Missouri	10,293
Montana	2,566
Nebraska	2,826
Nevada	3,143
New Hampshire	1,986

(Continued)

Table 10-2   (Continued)

New Jersey	13,515
New Mexico	6,635
New York	52,183
North Carolina	15,308
North Dakota	1,806
Ohio	19,115
Oklahoma	7,828
Oregon	6,807
Pennsylvania	21,796
Rhode Island	2,310
South Carolina	6,863
South Dakota	2,068
Tennessee	10,210
Texas	35,330
Utah	3,942
Vermont	1,671
Virginia	8,970
Washington	10,631
West Virginia	4,031
Wisconsin	9,556
Wyoming	2,214
Island areas:	0
American Samoa	180
Micronesia	98
Guam	342
Marshall Islands	136
Northern Marianas	128
Palau	23
Puerto Rico	6,135
Virgin Islands	302

Source: U.S. Census Bureau.

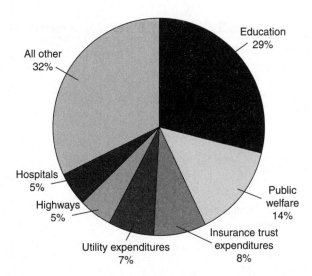

Figure 10-4   State and Local Government Expenditures, 2008 (*Source:* U.S. Census Bureau.)

Looking at these data as a whole, we see that state and local revenues were collected from a wide array of sources and expended on a vast range of projects. The sources of revenue give us some guide to the types of municipal bonds issued. In Table 10-3, we see an illustrative list that goes beyond the broad categories of taxes and intergovernmental transfers.

Each of these sources, either directly or indirectly, is a potential candidate for debt service payments on municipal bonds.

PENSIONS AND OTHER BENEFITS

The tendency of state and local governments to give their public-sector employees wages and benefits that are overly generous is well documented. In one striking example, the

Table 10-3   Typical Sources of State and Local Revenue

- University tuition
- School lunch sales
- Hospitals
- Highways
- Airports
- Parking facilities
- Port facilities
- Parks
- Community housing
- Sewage and solid waste
- Utility revenue, including water supply, electric power, and gas supply
- Transit
- Liquor store revenues
- Revenue from trusts

Source: Congressional Budget Office.

city of Vallejo, California, entered bankruptcy in order to gain relief from union contracts. Allegations of fraud are also common.

The lack of adequate disclosure of these benefits is a major problem. In July 2011, the Government Accounting Standards Board (GASB) moved to change the accounting for them. The heart of the problem is defined-benefit pension plans, which are common in the public sector but becoming rare in the private sector. Defined-benefit pension plans are those that define the amount of benefits employees receive after their employment ends. Different and far less onerous rules apply to defined-contribution plans, which identify the amount that is contributed to a retirement account dedicated to the employee.

GASB requires uniform methods of calculating the liabilities for pensions. The difference between the present value of the investments on hand and the projected liability is the unfunded liability. This unfunded liability must be reported on the balance sheet of the state or local government.

Moody's adds the unfunded liability to an issuer's bond indebtedness to get the total debt outstanding. This has a tendency to depress the ratings of governments that are not fully funding their retirement plans.

The state and local governments were often caught by surprise by the size of the liabilities. When the magnitude of the unfunded liabilities became known to the body politic, reform was initiated. In some cases, the pensions were changed from defined-benefit plans to a form of defined-contribution plans, at least for new employees. In one case, a state attempted to remove the collective bargaining rights of public employees.

The state pension problem is a complex multigenerational dilemma. From the accounting side, the Government Accountability Office (GAO) recommends a funding level of 80 percent or higher. A 2012 Pew Center report showed that 34 states had pension funds with less than the 80 percent funding ratio. The report estimated that the funding gap was on the order of $1 trillion. Other estimates place it higher.

The outrage of the accounting profession at the lack of disclosure and the method of calculations for public pensions has served to make the public aware of the problem, which in prior years it largely was not. State and local governments are now motivated to act. Between 2009 and 2011, 43 states have moved to control their pension liabilities. The general approaches were to reduce the cost of living adjustments, increase the contributions from workers, and reduce the benefits for current and future workers.

The policy side of the pension problem is acute as well. Fully funding pensions requires additional revenues. Higher taxes are possible, but it is far more likely that other programs will have to be cut. Looking at state and local budgets, the likely targets are education and other programs affecting the young. As a result, funding the plans is only one issue. That is within the capacity of the states to do, and it will be done. However, the intergenerational wealth transfer that is likely to result is at least as serious a problem as proper accounting.

Other postemployment benefits (OPEBs), such as retiree health benefits, will undoubtedly receive similar accounting and rating agency treatments. The same accounting and policy issues will be confronted as with the pensions.

11

The Yield Curve

If we return to the yields shown for the bonds on the front of the State of Illinois official statement (OS), we see that they have a smoothly rising structure (see Figure 3-7). The yields on the serial bonds rise consistently from 1.50 percent at a one-year maturity to 5.25 percent for a 20-year maturity. A set of yields like this, on bonds that are very similar but vary by maturity, is called a *yield curve*. Here we are ignoring the effect of the optional call on the bonds, a practice that is common in the industry.

These yields are in fact the yield curve for Illinois state general obligation bonds (GOs) on the date of issuance. See Figure 11-1. This is typical of municipal bond yield curves. It is strongly upward-sloping, rising fastest in the first years. The typical municipal bond yield curve flattens out for longer maturities.

Two features of the municipal tax-exempt yield curve are striking. First, the shape is unusual for a fixed-income

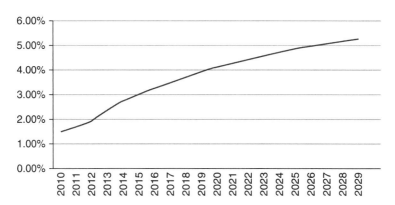

Figure 11-1   Illustrative Yield Curve (*Source:* Official statement for State of Illinois 2009 bonds.)

market. The spread between long- and short-maturity yields has been positive for decades, even when this was not true of the Treasury yield curve. The second interesting feature is the level of municipal bond yields relative to those for Treasuries. Because the municipal yields are not subject to federal tax, we would expect that in a perfect world, the municipal yield would equal the Treasury yield adjusted for taxes, or:

Municipal yield = (1 − marginal tax rate) × Treasury yield

If the marginal tax rate equaled 35 percent and the Treasury yield equaled 4 percent, we would expect the municipal bond yields to be 2.6 percent because the government would take 35 percent of the 4 percent, or 1.4 percent, from the Treasury yield.

Another way we can do the calculation is to compute the implied marginal tax rate. Suppose the municipal bond yield was actually 3.0 percent instead of 2.6 percent. Then

the ratio of municipal yields to Treasury yields would be
3.0/4.0 percent. Subtracting this from 1.0 gives us the
implied marginal tax rate of 25 percent.

In fact, implied marginal tax rates for municipal
money market yields are often close to the actual tax rate.
For longer maturities, however, the implied marginal tax
rate is far lower than the actual tax rate. In recent years, it
has been common for the ratio of yields on 30-year AAA
municipals to those on 30-year Treasuries to be well in
excess of 100 percent (see Figure 11-2). This would imply
a marginal tax rate for the municipal bond investor that is
negative.

The failure of implied marginal tax rates to equal the
actual tax rate in municipal bonds has been referred to as
the "muni puzzle." It has received extensive investigation in
the academic literature, but at this point it is far from having been resolved. The muni puzzle implies that an investor

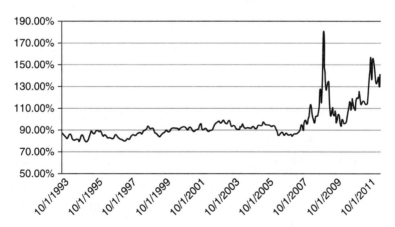

**Figure 11-2   30-Year Municipal/Treasury Ratios (*Source:*
Thomson Reuters Municipal Market Data and U.S. Treasury.)**

should be able to arbitrage between long and short maturities and earn a profit. This has not proved to be easy.

WHAT IS ARBITRAGE?

Some care must be used with the term *arbitrage,* as it has different meanings in different contexts. In the vernacular, people often talk loosely about engaging in arbitrage when they just mean buying and selling something.

In municipal bonds, the tax code defines an *arbitrage bond* as any bond that violates the tax rules with regard to the limitations on issuer arbitrage imposed by the IRS. These rules are lengthy and deal with differences in the yields of various bonds computed in ways that will make it difficult or impossible for a tax-exempt issuer to engage in tax arbitrage between the municipal market and taxable markets.

Arbitrage in economics arises when an investor makes an arbitrage profit. In classical economics, arbitrage is the process of buying and selling a single asset in two different markets, earning an instantaneous risk-free profit. This is often thought of in terms of buying gold in London at a low price and selling it in New York at a high price. In practice, this is rarely possible for an individual, but the classical example does contain merit.

Why would the price of gold be different in two markets? The asset is the same, gold. The prices are different, however, because of differential supply and demand for gold. As a result, arbitrage opportunities are available because of the character of the market, not the character of the asset.

In this way, arbitrage relies on features that are "endogenous" to the market. Arbitrageurs are not relying on an external event or announcement to make a profit. Instead, they are simply equalizing supply and demand for the asset and making money from the differences in market structure.

In practice, arbitrage is never truly risk-free. Modern notions of arbitrage involve trading similar assets to achieve an expected profit. In practice, arbitrage is usually a type of statistical arbitrage that varies with the bond and the exact nature of the market. These programs typically rely on rules-based procedures that provide trading signals. They do not depend upon a particular view about the asset being fundamentally rich or cheap.

Nor is the arbitrage profit supposed to depend upon the direction of prices in the market. The trade is designed to be market-neutral. In the bond market, market neutrality is generally achieved by having the trading position be interest-rate-neutral, which as a first estimate is "duration"-neutral. The arbitrage profit is not expected to be risk-free. There will be gains and losses over the course of time, but the average or expected return is positive. Arbitrage trading diversifies investments across markets and is expected to produce a relatively low-volatility return that is effectively uncorrelated with the market's return.

In fact, this description of statistical arbitrage captures the essential notion of municipal arbitrage done in tender option bond (TOB) programs. These programs are designed to be interest-rate-risk and credit-risk-neutral, relying on rules-based trading signals to learn the difference in interest rates on two similar assets. And excess returns are expected to be positive, that is, "statistical." TOB trades are explained in the last section of this chapter. However, numerous TOB programs have failed during financial panics, largely as a result of the collapse of the auction-rate market and the monoline insurer ratings.

TAX EFFICIENCY

The dilemma implicit in the muni puzzle is that the tax-exempt municipal bond market is expected to be efficient in an academic sense. This stems from the efficient market hypothesis, which was once business school dogma but is now widely questioned. It held that markets are informationally efficient and that any inefficiency is an anomaly.

Textbook definitions of efficiency usually rely on Eugene Fama's characterization of efficiency as weak form (prices have no memory), semi-strong form (you can't expect to make a profit on what's in the newspaper), and strong form (prices even know about secrets).

It is difficult, given the market failures of the Great Recession, to accept the bond markets as being efficient in any of these ways. It is doubtful that any market, especially the municipal market, is academically efficient. Even without the shocks of the Great Recession, the municipal bond market is replete with evidence of inefficiency. Efficiency relies on rational investors or well-capitalized arbitrageurs, both of which are in very short supply in the municipal market. Ironically, regulatory restrictions on tax arbitrage in the tax-exempt market may well have served to ensure tax inefficiency. Meaningful tax arbitrage by issuers and investors is illegal in municipals.

In addition, the informational efficiency of the market is inhibited by the operational efficiency of the market. The operational efficiency, or cost of trading, limits the informational efficiency. Price differences are a necessary condition for arbitrage in markets. An investor must be able to buy low and sell high. In addition, though, the investor must make a profit after costs from these transactions. Transaction costs are sometimes dismissed as being unimportant for arbitrage because of the use of derivatives like futures and swaps, which can have very low transaction costs. The municipal bond market, though, has tried and failed to construct a functional futures contract specifically because of the liquidity problems with the underlying bonds. The municipal swap market has also shown limited liquidity, especially in distressed markets.

Liquidity costs are important to investors. Most estimates of liquidity costs come from the secondary market, which is dominated by retail trades. Since most retail trades are buy and hold, those trades that do occur can be expected to be forced trades and not represent the true liquidity of institutional trades in the market.

Evidence for this comes from studies of the bid-asked spread for municipal trades reported in EMMA. The liquidity of a bond depends to a very large degree on the size of the trade. Spreads are large for retail trades but approach zero for institutionally sized trades. The bid-asked spread for a multimillion-dollar trade averages around 1 to 2 basis points (1/100 percent), while smaller trades can have a spread of a hundred basis points or more.

SEGMENTATION IN THE MUNICIPAL MARKET

The municipal market can best be understood as a collection of micromarkets that are poorly arbitraged. The micromarkets are separated by a number of factors. Different state tax treatments for in- and out-of-state bonds tend to isolate the state markets. Federal tax treatment divides the market into bank-eligible bonds and others. There are also distinct pricing features for alternative minimum tax (AMT) bonds. And the list goes on. The structure of the bond is also important. Institutional and retail buyers have different preferences in terms of coupon and maturity (preferred habitats).

Figure 11-3 gives visual insight into the structure of the secondary market for municipal bonds. It shows the number of trades and the par amounts traded for a single day.

As we can see, about 80 percent of the trades occur for the smallest category of par amounts, $0–$100,000. On the other end of the spectrum, the $1,000,000+ trades,

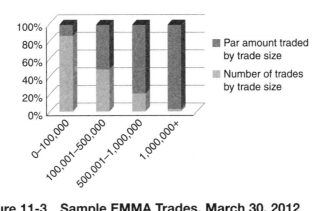

Figure 11-3   Sample EMMA Trades, March 30, 2012
(*Source:* SIFMA.)

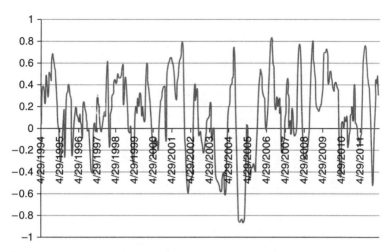

Figure 11-4   Correlation of Long- and Short-Term Tax-Exempt Rates (*Source:* Federal Reserve.)

which occurred 3 percent of the time, accounted for about 69 percent of the par amount traded that day.

Evidence of segmentation of tax-exempt yields by maturity can be seen in Figure 11-4, which shows rolling 30-week correlations between the short-term SIFMA swap rate and the long-term Bond Buyer 20 Index.

The Bond Buyer 20 Index consists of 20 high-grade GOs with 20-year maturities. It is representative of the average yield on a long-term, high-grade, tax-exempt bond portfolio.

The average correlation of these two indexes is 0.13, not much different from zero. In addition, the correlations swing in a noisy pattern from about 0.8 to −0.8, suggesting a close-to-impossible trading relationship.

Finally, we can look at the relationship of long-term taxable and tax-exempt rates, as seen in Figure 11-5.

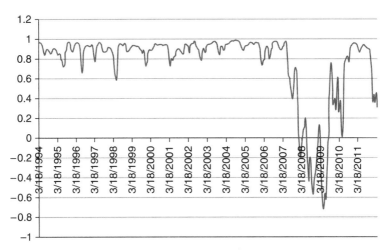

Figure 11-5   Long Bond Treasury/Municipal Yield Correlation
(*Source:* **Federal Reserve.)**

Here we show 30 rolling weekly correlations between 30-year AAA GO and 30-year Treasury bond yields. While this is most assuredly not a perfect correlation, the rates were generally correlated in the 80–90 percent range until the financial panics of 2007 and 2008. The low correlations at the end of the series suggest that the markets were still highly perturbed in 2012.

TENDER OPTION BONDS

A tender option bond is an investment vehicle that arbitrages the long and short ends of the municipal bond market. It involves taking bond coupons that would have been sold on the long end of the municipal yield curve and selling them instead in the tax-exempt money market. The TOB device includes a grantor trust that preserves the tax-exempt nature of the interest passing through it.

Essentially, a bond is placed in a trust, and most of the cash flows from the trust go to a floating-rate money market instrument, the "floater"; the remainder go to a residual certificate. The floaters trade like other money market instruments. The trust hires a broker/dealer to serve as remarketing agent for the floater. In the event that no buyer is found, the floater is put to a liquidity provider, such as a bank. The maturity of the put, which is usually seven days, is under SEC rules; this is the effective maturity of the floater rather than the long maturity of the bonds in the TOB trust.

TOBs are passive investments that do not tranche or divide up the credit of the underlying bond. In this sense, they function like a repo in providing financing in the municipal bond market.

Tender option bonds generate floaters, which have accounted for about 25 to 30 percent of tax-exempt money fund assets. These floaters are municipal money market fund securities meeting the requirements of Rule 2a-7 of the Investment Company Act. Rule 2a-7 requires that the money fund assets be primarily high grade and highly liquid. This rule has been revised numerous times. The status of bank-initiated TOBs is subject to review under the proposed Volcker Rule.

12

Municipal Bond
Yield Calculations

This chapter presents the relationship between bond prices and yields. First, the fundamental concept of bond interest is presented. This is followed by a discussion of the different types of yields and then a demonstration from several Bloomberg calculators.

WHAT IS INTEREST?

Interest is the return on lending money. That is true enough, but, as my first professors in finance impressed on me, it is more easily understood as the rental cost of money. Renting anything has a cost. How is the cost determined? From the perspective of the person who wants to rent an object to earn income, he must earn enough on the transaction to induce the investment in the first place. In other words, the person putting something up for rent has to get enough from the process of renting to cause him to give up some form of consumption like taking a vacation with the money and instead buy and rent out a lawn mower.

Economists refer to this return from a deferral of consumption as the *real rate of return*. The real rate of return changes over time, but it is usually expected to be about 3 percent, ignoring taxes and other fees. And although it changes over time, it usually has a low volatility.

There is another part of the renter's arithmetic. When the lawn mower is rented out, it inevitably comes back in worse shape. It is depreciated as a result of the use. Money can depreciate too, and usually does. The value of money tends to decline over time relative to that of real assets like lawn mowers or loaves of bread. We refer to this decline in the purchasing power of money as *inflation*. Inflation is a kind of depreciation.

The renter of the lawn mower needs to charge enough to be compensated both for deferring consumption and for depreciation. This is exactly what the money lender does when it lends out its capital.

As a first approximation, we can write that the rate of interest on a loan is equal to the sum of the real rate of return and the rate of inflation. Of course, the lender cannot know the future, so he must charge for the *expected* real rate and the *expected* inflation. In these examples, we will hold the real rate constant and concentrate on the impact of expected inflation.

Yield = real rate of interest + expected inflation

If the real rate of interest is 3 percent and the expected rate of inflation is 4 percent, then the market yield per year should be 7 percent (3 percent + 4 percent). Unless otherwise stated, yields and returns are assumed to be annual.

Going from interest rates to dollars of interest requires the use of a calculator. Each type of security has its own specific formula. In general, though, there are three types of calculations that convert an interest rate to an interest payment in dollars. Simple interest calculations are, as the name implies, the simplest. Here the dollars of interest are equal to the principal times the interest rate times the term of the loan. A 5 percent loan of $100 due in two years will pay $10 (0.05 × $100 × 2 years) in interest at the end of two years.

The interest due after one year is half this amount, or $5. In simple interest calculations, there was no interest earned on the $5 during the last year of the loan. With compound interest, there is interest on the interest, and this accrues at specific discrete times. Bond calculations typically employ compound interest. Finally, there is a mathematical idea of interest compounding instantaneously over time. This type of continuous interest is contained in some option-pricing calculations.

TYPES OF BOND YIELDS

Now we will switch our discussion to bonds, where the interest earned is called the *yield*. It is important to say at the outset that bonds are traded for dollar prices. In a transaction to buy or sell a bond, by far the most important thing is how many dollars will be exchanged. In each transaction, there will be only one price. That price can produce many different types of yields, depending on what formula is used.

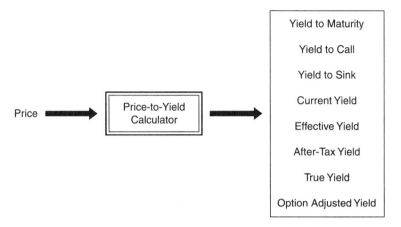

Figure 12-1   Price/Yield Conversion

As Figure 12-1 shows, there is only one price at which a bond is purchased or sold. For example, one bond may sell at a price of 101.02, and another bond may sell at a price of 103.00. Some bonds are quoted in dollar amounts like this. These "dollar bonds" are often not paying interest and are said to be trading "flat." This is unusual, however, since the vast majority of bonds are quoted in yields. Comparing the bonds based on their computed yields is far more convenient than dealing with the prices of the instruments themselves.

The problem is that we need to choose exactly which calculator we are going to use in order to produce the yield. Different investors can have very different ideas about what will occur in the future. A bond can have optional calls, sink dates, put dates, and many other options. Each of these produces different possible cash flows in the future for the investor.

For example, if the bond is called, the investor receives coupons only until the call date, when the call premium and face value are paid. On the other hand, the investor could receive coupons until the stated maturity date and then the return of principal. If we use a calculator that assumes that the cash flows will continue only to the call date, we will get the yield to call. If we assume the other case, in which all of the cash flows continue to maturity, the calculator will produce the yield to maturity.

Which yield do we use? That is dictated by market convention and regulation. The general rule is that the broker/dealer will report the "yield to worst" to the investor. We first compute the yield to maturity and the yield to each call date. The investor is quoted the lowest of the yields, which is the yield to worst. So, if the yield to maturity is 5 percent and the yield to call is 6 percent, the yield to worst is the yield to maturity, 5 percent.

The yield quoted to the investor at the time of purchase is sometimes called the *promised yield*. What the investor actually gets as a return on her investment will depend on what cash flows are actually paid and the path of future interest rates. The investor, for example, may be quoted a yield that assumes that the bond goes to maturity when in fact the bond is called after a few years, producing a return for the investor that is far different from the yield that was promised when the bond was purchased. The yield here is promised only as an economic expectation, not as a legal contract. An investor cannot sue to get the yield offered when the bond was purchased.

The types of yields listed in Figure 12-1 are just a sample of those that can be produced mathematically. Most of them employ present value techniques. One major exception is the current yield. The current yield is a convenient measure, but it can be very misleading. It is simply the coupon on the bond divided by the bond's price. If the bond has a 5 percent coupon and a price of 90, its current yield is 5.56 percent $(0.05/90 \times 100)$.

The effective yield on the bond employs a variable reinvestment rate for the coupons. If the coupons are reinvested at the bond's yield, the effective yield is equal to the yield to maturity. If they are reinvested at rates higher than the bond's yield, the effective yield is higher than the yield to maturity on the bond, and vice versa.

The after-tax yield is equal to multiplying the pretax yield by one minus the investor's marginal tax rate:

After-tax yield = pretax yield × (1 − marginal tax rate)

If the investor is paying a 35 percent tax rate and buys a fully taxable bond with a 5 percent yield, then the tax will be 1.75 percent (0.35×5 percent), leaving the investor with an after-tax yield of 3.25 percent. This is equivalent to multiplying the pretax yield by one minus the tax rate, or 3.25 percent [(5 percent $\times (1 - 0.35)$)].

The process can be inverted by dividing the after-tax yield by one minus the marginal tax rate to obtain the pretax equivalent yield. In the previous example, dividing the after-tax yield of 3.25 percent by one minus the marginal tax rate $(1 - 0.35)$ gives us the pretax equivalent yield of 5 percent.

In computing the pretax equivalent yield, some care needs to be made to use the true after-tax yield. The after-tax yield may be different from the stated yield for a "tax-exempt" municipal bond if the bond is subject to the alternative minimum tax (AMT) or market discount taxes that would lower the amount of yield the buyer of a municipal bond would receive.

The true yield uses the standard yield-to-worst calculations except that it uses the exact day on which the investor receives the funds. The standard calculations assume that coupons and other cash flows are paid at regular intervals, usually semiannually. However, the regular payment date could be on a weekend or a legal holiday, which means that the investor will actually receive the money on the next business day, later than the model assumes, thus lowering the yield that is actually received. For long-term bonds, the effect is usually small, but with notes, the true yield can be considerably lower than the yield to maturity.

The last type of yield that we will present here is the option-adjusted yield. An option is the right but not the obligation to buy or sell a security at a given price within a specified time. A municipal bond contains a variety of options. The most common type to be considered in option-adjusted yield calculations is the issuer's optional call. Around 90 percent of newly issued municipal bonds contain calls of this type.

Although many types of calls exist in the market, the par call with 10 years of call protection is the typical municipal bond call. In this type of call, the issuer reserves the right to call the security away from the investor and stop paying interest on a bond after it has been outstanding for 10 years. Usually there is no call premium, so that the price paid to the investor on the call date is merely par. The call is embedded in a tax-exempt bond, and tax regulations effectively prohibit stripping it away from the bond and selling it separately.

Because the option is embedded in the bond, it is usually not appropriate to use an everyday option calculation like the Black-Scholes model. These models use constant price volatility for the instrument that underlies the call. With long-term bonds, however, the volatility of the instrument will decline to zero as the instrument approaches maturity. This demands that more complicated models be employed.

The underlying idea, without regard to exactly which model is employed, is that the price of the bond with the call should be equal to the value of the bond without the call minus the value of the call. Valuation is done from the bond-holder's perspective. It is as though the bondholder purchased a noncallable bond and then sold a call option to the issuer. As a result, the bondholder is long (holds) the non-callable bond and is short (has sold) the call option to the issuer. Essentially, this is one equation and can have only one unknown. This is shown in the next formula:

Whole bond price = noncallable bond value − call value

If we know the price of the bond that is being offered in the market, which is the usual case, and we can calculate the value of the call, we can use arithmetic to compute the value of the noncallable bond. Suppose that the whole bond trades for a price of 101 and the call is worth 5 points; the noncallable bond is then worth 106. From this set of prices, we can identify the yield on the noncallable bond. The noncallable yield then allows us to find the interest-rate spread over the AAA yield curve to satisfy our equation. The adjustment is, in one way or another, the option-adjusted spread, or OAS. The OAS tells the investor how much he is receiving for the credit risk on the bond. If, for example, the OAS is 50 basis points (0.5 percent) and the market requires 40 basis points (0.4 percent), then the bond is cheap relative to other bonds in the market.

The calculation of the option value varies by model. Generally, the risk-free yield curve and an estimate of the volatility of yields in the market are required inputs. These are used to estimate the possible future paths of interest rates.

It is important to remember that these models do not set the price of the bond in the market. That is set by supply and demand for the bond. However, one can use a model to attempt to estimate the fair price of the bond.

Ideally, there are enough actively priced callable and noncallable bonds in the market to allow us to directly observe the inputs to these models. The computations of these option models can be very complex, making the reliability of the inputs especially important. For example, estimates of volatility are often based on the volatility of options on LIBOR. In practice, it is common for trading desks to apply a haircut to (lower) these estimates until the model gives an option value that they think is reasonable given the conditions in the market.

If used properly, OAS models can be useful relative-value tools. Given two bonds with similar structures—that is, call provisions, coupons, and maturities—the models can be a guide as to how one bond should be priced relative to the other. These models, like their mathematically complex cousins in other markets, need to be used recognizing their limitations. This is especially troublesome for tax-exempt municipal bonds.

One of the primary problems with the standard academic models used for tax-exempt bonds is that municipal bonds contain many types of options, not just optional calls. Models need to take into account advance refunding, market discount tax, sinking funds, and other municipal bond–specific features before we can expect them to provide specific guidance on a bond's absolute value.

PRICE SENSITIVITY

What happens to the price of a bond when yields change? Let's think about bank deposits for a minute. How much would you pay to receive $100 one year from now if the bank was paying 10 percent per year? That is its market price. The $100 paid by the bank has two parts: interest and principal. One year from now, the investor gets the interest on the deposit as well as a return of the amount invested (the principal):

Principal invested + interest earned on the principal
= $100 paid by the bank at the end of the year

We can see that if we deposited $90.91 now, we would get $9.09 in interest (90.91 × 0.1), for a total of $100.

This bank deposit is just one way in which the bank can borrow $90.91. The bank could sell another type of security, a note, to the public. In that case, the 10 percent interest rate would be the yield on a note issued by the bank for a market price of $90.91.

Yields can increase or decrease over time as circumstances and expectations change. Suppose that the yield on the note went to 12 percent; in that case, $89.29 would be enough to earn $100 in a year because the bank would pay $10.71 (89.29 × 0.12). Again, the principal plus the interest on the principal would equal $100. The opposite is true as well: falling yields cause bond prices to rise. The general principle, then, is that bond prices move inversely with bond yields.

The rate at which bond prices change as yields move is referred to formally as the *duration* of the bond. We can get a very rough notion of what duration means with the example just given. When bond yields rose 2 percent, from 10 percent to 12 percent, prices declined from $90.91 to $89.29. The sensitivity of bond price to changes in bond yield can be expressed as the percent change in price divided by the change in yield:

Sensitivity = percent price change/yield change

Percent price change = (90.91 − 89.29)/90.91
= 1.78 percent

Yield change, percent = 2 percent

Sensitivity = 1.78 percent/2 percent = 0.89

This is one type of price sensitivity to yield. The value, 0.89, has a unit associated with it: years. The price sensitivity (effective duration) is 0.89 year. Price sensitivities are stated as positive numbers even though their strictly calculated value is negative, reflecting the inverse relationship of price and yield changes with bonds.

The larger the maturity, or duration, the more sensitive the price is to changes in yields. However, price sensitivities for coupon bonds are not linear with maturity. That is, doubling the maturity of the bond does not double the duration. This is a result of the mathematics of bond pricing.

Durations are first approximations of price changes in response to changes in yield. They are, in a sense, the velocity of bond pricing. The duration provides an estimate of the amount of price change when yields change. However, it is just an estimate, and the bond price may be higher or lower than the duration suggests. If the actual bond price is higher than the estimate, the bond is said to have *positive convexity*. If it is lower, the bond is said to have *negative convexity*. Negative convexity is associated with embedded calls in bonds. In addition, it is important to tax-adjust durations when one deals with municipal bonds.

Taxes, especially market discount taxes, make discount tax-exempt bonds more sensitive to rising rates than the standard duration calculations imply. Rising yields, for example, increase the taxes due on the bond. This adds to the decline in price resulting from discounting the bond cash flows by a higher yield.

Now let's look at a pair of Bloomberg calculators for tax-exempt bonds.

The first screen, FTAX (Figure 12-2), shows the impact of the market discount tax on bond cash flow. For calculation

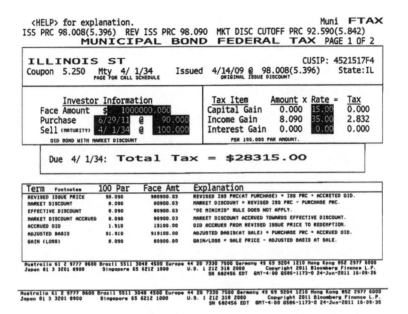

Figure 12-2 Bloomberg FTAX Calculator (*Source:* Bloomberg L.P. Used with permission of Bloomberg L.P. Copyright © 2012. All rights reserved.)

purposes, the calculator employs the rule that the accretion of the market discount is ordinary income and that the tax is presumed to be paid at maturity.

Here an Illinois state bond with a 5.25 percent coupon and a maturity of 4/1/2034 is analyzed. The bond was purchased on 6/29/2011 for a price of 90 percent of face value. The prevailing tax rates are 15 percent for capital gains and 35 percent for income. Coupon income is taxed at zero because this is a tax-exempt municipal bond.

The bond was issued at a price of 98.008 and a yield of 5.396 percent. Since the original issue yield is more than the coupon rate, the bond was sold at a discount when it was originally issued. As a result, it is an original issue discount (OID). The accretion of the bond price from 98.008 to par at maturity for an OID is interest, and since it is a tax-exempt bond, the interest is tax-exempt.

The first step in the analysis is to compute the price the bond would have now at the new-issue yield. This is the *accreted price*. On this screen, the accreted price is called the "revised issue price" and is equal to the original issue price plus the accretion. In this case, the revised issue price is 98.090. If the bond had been issued at par or at an original issue premium, the amount of the market discount would have been 100 minus the purchase price. In this case, however, the amount of market discount is the revised issue price less the purchase price, or 8.09 points (98.090 − 90.000).

The market discount rule does not apply if the size of the market discount is small. As mentioned earlier, "small" in Latin is *de minimis*. There are a variety of de minimis rules in the tax code, and this one applies only to the market discount rule. The tax code defines "small" for discount purposes as a discount less than 0.25 point times the number of full years to maturity. A full year is the truncated number of years to maturity.

A bond with a remaining maturity of 10.99 years has 10 full years to maturity. In this case, the bond has 22.77 years to maturity. The bond has a de minimis limit of 5.5 points (22 × 0.25). The market discount cutoff is 98.09 less 5.50, or 92.59. If the bond price were within de minimis, or less than 92.59, the market discount rule would not apply.

This doesn't mean that there would be no tax on the accretion of the discount. Instead, the accretion would be taxed as a capital gain.

In this case, the discount of 8.09 is greater than the market discount cutoff of 5.50 points. As a result, the bond is said to be outside of de minimis, and the discount will be taxed as ordinary income.

The amount of the ordinary income tax is 35 percent times the discount of 8.09, or 2.83 points. If the principal amount is $1 million, the tax due at the maturity of the bond on 4/1/2034 will be $28,315. This is shown in the center of the screen.

These calculations show how to adjust the cash flow for a market discount bond. There are a variety of other tax calculations, but they are contained within this framework.

If the bond is a discount bond but within de minimis, the accreted interest is a capital gain. It can be a long-term capital gain if the holding period is more than a year. Then the gain will be subject to the special long-term capital gains rate of 15 percent. If the holding period is one year or less, the gain is treated as ordinary income. The rules are laid out in IRS Publication 550:

Holding Period

If you sold or traded investment property, you must determine your holding period for the property. Your holding period determines whether any capital gain or loss was a short-term or a long-term capital gain or loss.

Long-term or short-term. If you hold investment property more than 1 year, any capital gain or loss is a long-term capital gain or loss. If you hold the property 1 year or less, any capital gain or loss is a short-term capital gain or loss.

To determine how long you held the investment property, begin counting on the date after the day you acquired the property. The day you disposed of the property is part of your holding period.

Example

If you bought investment property on February 3, 2010, and sold it on February 3, 2011, your holding period is not more than 1 year and you have a short-term capital gain or loss. If you sold it on February 4, 2011, your holding period is more than 1 year and you have a long-term capital gain or loss.

Securities traded on an established market.

For securities traded on an established securities market, your holding period begins the day after the trade date you bought the securities, and ends on the trade date you sold them.

The tax treatment of capital gains for premium bonds is similar except that the amortization of the premium is not a taxable event for municipal bonds. That is, if one buys a bond at 105 and yields in the market remain the same, the bond will amortize down in price as time passes. Suppose that it amortizes to a price of 104; the price decline from 105 to 104 is not a capital loss for tax calculations.

PRICE/YIELD CALCULATOR

Now we can look at pricing a bond using the standard Bloomberg price/yield screen, YA, shown in Figure 12-3.

Here we have the same Illinois bond used in our earlier example. Now we have a settlement date of 4/17/2011 and a price of 90. Buying the bond under these conditions produces a cost at settlement of $902,333.33, which is shown in the bottom panel. Next to it is the income expected to be received on the bond if all the coupons are reinvested to maturity.

Yields are computed to maturity and to worst (the lower of yield to call and yield to maturity). Since this is a discount bond, the yield to worst and the yield to maturity are the same.

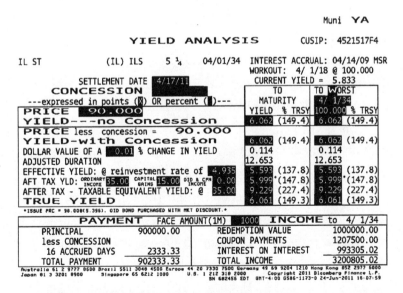

Figure 12-3   Bloomberg YA Screen (*Source:* Bloomberg L.P. Used with permission of Bloomberg L.P. Copyright © 2012. All rights reserved.)

The easiest yield calculation is the current yield, the coupon divided by the price. This is 5.833 (5.25/0.90). The dollar value of 0.01 is the price impact of moving the yield on the bond 1 basis point, or 0.114 point. The adjusted duration, 12.653 years, is the modified duration, the effect of instantaneously moving the yield curve 100 basis points (bp). These price sensitivity measures do not take taxes into account. A market discount bond is more price-sensitive than a par or premium bond.

Several variations on the computation of the yield to maturity are given. The yield without any tax adjustments, and assuming that the coupons are reinvested to maturity, is 6.062 percent per year. Again, unless stated otherwise, the yields are always annualized.

If the coupons are reinvested at rates higher or lower than the yield on the bond, the effective yield will be higher or lower than the yield to maturity given in the YA screen. If the coupons are reinvested at 4.935 percent, the bondholder can expect to receive a yield to maturity of 5.593 percent instead of the yield to worst, 6.062 percent.

This bond is an OID with market discount, so there is tax due on the bond. A tax calculation like the one shown in the FTAX screen in Figure 12-2 must be done. The tax due is subtracted from the coupon and principal payment that the bondholder will receive at maturity. The internal rate of return that causes the discounted present value of the after-tax cash flows to equal the price of the bond is the after-tax yield (AFT TAX YLD). Here it is 5.999 percent. This is less than the yield to maturity and reflects the fact that part of the yield is going to be paid to the IRS.

The payment to the IRS is reflected in the price and comes out of the amount that the current bondholder receives from the sale of the bond. The purchaser demands that he be paid the tax because it is assumed that he will be required to pay the tax at maturity. Bonds that are close to becoming market discounts are discounted heavily in the market.

The taxable equivalent yield is the bond's after-tax yield divided by 1 minus the marginal tax rate. We have seen in the FTAX calculations that computing the tax on a muni bond can be quite tedious, but it must be done. The bond should be bought or sold only on the basis of the after-tax yield. And, the taxable equivalent yield must use the after-tax yield. The taxable equivalent yield in this case is 9.229 percent [5.999/(1 − 0.35)].

Finally, the true yield is computed, which adjusts for holidays and weekends. The true yield on the bond is 6.061 percent, close to the yield to maturity. For long-term bonds, the difference between the true yield and the yield to maturity is typically small. For notes, however, that may not be true, and the true yield is a very important calculation.

13

Elements of Portfolio Structuring

At this point, we are in the position of designing municipal bond portfolios. The bonds employed here will be tax-
exempt unless otherwise specified. The basic idea is that
effective portfolio structuring in bonds requires a sense of
why a particular bond is being acquired. In some cases, it
is to hedge a position for a day. But often it is to fund a
future liability. Individuals buy bonds to fund their retirement, and issuers buy bonds to defease debt service. In these
cases, there is a target horizon value that the investor is seeking. Sometimes the horizon date is indefinite, as when an
individual is investing for wealth generation.

Each of these involves slightly different approaches. We
will start with discussing portfolio risk and return.

PORTFOLIO RISK AND RETURN

A portfolio's return and risk are a function of the bonds in
the portfolio, of course. The return of a portfolio is the market

value–weighted average return of the bonds in the portfolio. If the portfolio has two bonds, one with $100 in market value and the other with $200 in market value, the weights are 1/3 (100/300) and 2/3 (200/300). If the first one returns 6 percent and the other one 9 percent, the portfolio's return is 8 percent [(1/3 × 6) + (2/3 × 9)].

The risk measures are more complex. The standard measure for risk in the capital asset pricing model (CAPM) is the standard deviation of the portfolio. The standard deviation is a function of the variances and covariance of the returns for the constituent bonds. The calculation can be tedious but is necessary.

In practice, the CAPM has had limited application in municipal bonds because it is inherently a single-period model. The analysis begins and ends in one period, usually a year. This often does not capture a bond problem, since most bonds are multiperiod or long-term.

One alternative measure of risk is the difference between the expected horizon value and the realized value. If one is investing to fund a college education in 20 years, the return in the first year is only one-twentieth of the problem. The amount available in 20 years, not the amount at the end of year 1, is the most relevant issue. Risk in this sense is the chance that the horizon value will be less than the required amount, not just the volatility of the annual returns.

One approach to reducing the horizon risk is to immunize the investment against changes in future interest rates. Immunization implies that, no matter what future interest rates do, the investor will get the expected future value from the bond. In practice, few things can be exactly immunized.

Here we will use the duration of the assets and liabilities to get an approximate immunization.

Coupon management is one challenge with immunization. With a coupon bond, the realized return rises and falls with future interest rates, and coupon management is a critical component of the strategy. Let's take an example. Suppose we have a simple 5 percent, 30-year bond. This consists of an annuity of $25 for 60 periods from the semi-annual coupon payments plus the face value of $1,000 at maturity. At maturity, the investment will have produced approximately $3,400, of which $2,400 will have come from the coupons and the interest earned by the coupons if they are reinvested at 5 percent. That is, more than 70 percent of the return comes from the coupons and coupon reinvestment. But, this requires that the coupons be managed.

The simplest procedure for minimizing the coupon management problems is to use tax-exempt zero-coupon bonds. The duration of a zero-coupon bond is equal to its maturity. So, buying a zero-coupon bond to pay off a single future liability is equivalent to matching the duration of the asset to the duration of the liability.

There are no income taxes to consider because if the zero-coupon bond is purchased in the primary market, it is an OID, and the accretion of the OID is tax-exempt interest. This would not be true, of course, in the case of a taxable municipal bond. And if the tax-exempt zero is purchased in the secondary market, any discount in excess of the remaining OID would be taxable.

Another approach to managing the risk of a multiperiod liability is a variation on this immunization concept: cash matching. If the future liability has a series of cash flows, a portfolio that produces exactly matching cash flows serves to immunize the liability.

ISSUER CASH MATCHING

The most common way in which cash matching is used in municipal bonds is the defeasance of an advance refunded bond. The issuer will generally want to defease, or legally retire, an outstanding bond. If the issuer performs a legal defeasance, the liability is removed from the issuer's books. Alternatively, the issuer may create an investment portfolio that, for all intents and purposes, meets the debt service due on an outstanding bond.

This may constitute an economic defeasance, but it does not remove the outstanding bond as a liability of the issuer. One reason that a cash match may be an economic defeasance but not a legal defeasance is that the quality of the investments may be too low.

One straightforward cash-matching procedure for a state or local issuer is to buy zero-coupon bonds that exactly match the amount and timing of the coupons and the face amount coming due on an outstanding bond, the refunded bond. Since the issuer is tax-exempt, taxes on the investment would not be a factor.

Logically, the issuer would want to use the cheapest or highest-yielding zero-coupon bonds. In the past, this nearly always involved employing taxable bonds, especially zero-coupon Treasury bonds. And that is exactly what issuers did for many years. They were able to buy Treasury zeros and coupons at yields high enough to legally defease the outstanding debt service and pay for the underwriting cost of the refunding. The difference between the cost of the defeasance portfolio of Treasuries and the debt service on the refunded bond was pocketed as an arbitrage profit to the issuer.

Today, that is not possible. In order for a bond to be tax-exempt, it cannot be an "arbitrage bond." Issuers must meet the yield restrictions of the Internal Revenue Code. These are extensive and complex. Generally, the proceeds of a tax-exempt bond cannot be invested at yields that are "materially higher" than the borrowing cost. In many cases, this means that the yield on the investments made with money from any kind of municipal bond sale, such as power bonds, cannot exceed the yield on the bond by more than 1/8 percent.

In addition, advance refundings have special and much tighter rules. Only bonds that are not private-purpose bonds (governmental-purpose bonds) can be advance refunded, and those only once. In addition, the yield on the defeasance portfolio and the refunded bond's debt service has severe limits. In general, the yield on the refunding escrow cannot exceed the yield on the refunding bond by more than 1/1000 of one percentage point.

As a result of these rules, an issuer that wishes to advance refund an outstanding bond can build a portfolio that cash-matches and thus defeases the debt service on the old refunded bond, but it cannot earn an arbitrage profit. If the issuer does earn arbitrage, it must rebate it to the Treasury.

Until very recently, long-term municipal bond yields were around 80–90 percent of Treasuries. So if the issuer wanted to buy a zero-coupon Treasury bond to put in the escrow fund, it would have to knock its yield down. If the municipal bond to be defeased had a yield of 5 percent and the Treasury bond had a yield of 6 percent, the issuer would be able to receive only about a 5 percent yield from the Treasury. This was a problem because another Treasury rule required the issuer to buy the bond at a market rate.

This led to a serious violation of Treasury rules in which some underwriters illegally sold issuers Treasuries at a 5 percent yield. This markup in price (markdown in yield) became known as "yield burning" and led to numerous investigations.

The way out of this conundrum was to have the Treasury mark up the bonds for state and local governments to buy. A special, nonmarketable Treasury series is available for that purpose: the State and Local Government (SLG) Series. State and local governments can apply to the Treasury to buy zero-coupon Treasuries maturing in the amounts and on the days required for the state or local government's investment needs. The yields are set low enough for the issuer to comply with the yield restrictions of the no-arbitrage rules and are never higher than yields for Treasuries trading in the secondary market.

What happens if, as is common now, municipal bond yields are higher than Treasuries'? The arbitrage rules still apply, limiting the issuer to essentially zero positive arbitrage. There is no regulatory limit the other way, however. The issuer may be allowed by Treasury regulations to structure an escrow with a yield as high as 5 percent in our example, but the market may provide only bonds with a yield of 3 percent. In that case, there is a negative arbitrage of 2 percent.

For the issuer, this negative arbitrage is a cost that must be netted against any interest-rate savings provided by the refunding. For example, it is common for the issuer to be required to save from 2 to 3 percent of the face value of the refunding bond in an advance refunding. If the issuer has an outstanding bond of $10,000,000, a 2 percent savings is $200,000 in interest cost savings between the present value of the debt service costs of the refunding and refunded bonds. But after the negative arbitrage of the escrow is subtracted, along with underwriting costs, from the gross interest-rate savings, the refunding savings may not be enough to justify the advance refunding. This is true even with an apparently large reduction in coupons paid by the issuer on the outstanding bond.

With negative arbitrage, advance refundings but not current refundings will fall. But even current refundings occur less frequently than many investors expect. Most municipal bonds are small issues. This can lead to the issuer failing to even currently refund an issue when interest rates fall because the absolute dollar amount to be gained, after adjusting for regulatory and transaction costs, does not warrant the refunding.

Issuers do act to save taxpayers money by refunding appropriate bonds even with negative arbitrage. In practice, underwriters use optimization models to find the best combination of issues for the refunding escrow that provides the highest yield allowed for the issuer. Coupon bonds are frequently chosen when they are cheaper than zeros.

As mentioned in Chapter 6, the defeased refunded bond is now called a pre-re. Investors in pre-res need to be very conscious of the composition of the escrow, since that is what they are buying. Often federal agency securities and other taxable issues are in the refunding escrow. These pre-res trade at lower prices than pre-res with 100 percent Treasuries. Investors should buy a pre-re only at prices that are appropriate to the composition of the escrow.

The Treasury arbitrage rules do not place any restrictions on the escrow yield of taxable municipal bonds. And though it would be unusual, tax-exempt bonds have been used to advance refund other tax-exempt bonds. It is even possible to have pre-res in the advance refunding escrow of other bonds.

NONISSUER STRATEGIES

Advance refunding escrows are a special case of cash matching and immunization strategies used by issuers. Individuals can also cash-match a series of liabilities, but this has its problems. The zero market in tax-exempts is relatively thin, especially in shorter maturities. Individuals are not allowed to buy SLGs. As a result, zeros of a particular state, maturity, and rating are often not available at a cost-effective level. Most of the municipal bond market consists of fixed-coupon bonds, and here a different sense of immunization is required from that used with zero-coupon bonds.

Short Horizons

Bond portfolio management requires a definition of the holding period. For risk managers at broker/dealers and bond traders, the horizon can be very short. Positions are marked to market at least daily, so instantaneous bond-price sensitivities are important. The modified duration of a bond is the percentage price change for an instantaneous yield move of 100 basis points (bp). And, it is a useful first approximation of the price sensitivity of a bond to a sudden yield shift. The yield curve is assumed to make a parallel shift. The durations can be calculated in Excel or obtained from a broker.

Immunizing a municipal bond portfolio with a short horizon generally involves matching the duration of the municipal bond portfolio with that of one or more hedge instruments. The duration of a portfolio is, like the return of the portfolio, the market value–weighted average duration of the bonds in the portfolio.

Conceptually, matching the durations of the asset and of the hedge portfolio is relatively straightforward. The problem is estimating the yield betas. The yield beta equates the yield movement of the asset with that of the hedge.

The tax code makes direct shorting of tax-exempt municipal bonds extremely difficult. The interest paid on the debt of a municipality is tax-exempt. However, when a person borrows a municipal bond and sells it, creating a short position, the seller must pay the buyer interest on the bond. Because the seller is not a municipality, the buyer gets taxable interest, which would probably not be attractive to a buyer of tax-exempt municipal bonds.

Immunizing, or hedging, the municipal bond portfolio requires that the dollar change in the municipal portfolio be offset by an exact change in the dollar amount of the hedge, which we will consider to be a Treasury portfolio.

The Treasuries are, in one way or another, sold short so that a rise in yield produces a gain, whereas a rise in yield on a long position in municipal bonds will produce a loss. If municipal bond and Treasury yields moved in perfect unison, hedging in this way would be easy. Unfortunately, the relationship between changes in municipal and Treasury yields, or the yield beta, becomes extremely difficult to predict during periods of market disruption.

Longer Horizons

Most investors have holding periods that are measured in years. The problem becomes one of how to use coupon bonds to achieve an immunization of a longer-term liability. The size and timing of the liability controls the problem. With zero-coupon bonds, the basic rule is to set the duration of the asset equal to the duration of the liability. This is simplified because the duration of a zero-coupon bond or a single liability is its maturity. It is often cheaper to use coupon bonds rather than zeros. But, the rule is the same: match durations.

Defining the holding period is an essential element of bond risk management. If the goal is to achieve a horizon value equal to a long-term liability, short-term movement in interest rates is only one factor in the problem. If interest rates spike immediately after the purchase, all is not lost.

The popular notions about bond risk often forget the problems that the bonds are being used to solve. If one buys a 30-year bond and interest rates suddenly rise, the price of the bond will fall. No investor likes to see his assets decline in value. What is often forgotten, though, is that the value of the liability has also dropped, and if the durations are approximately the same, the investor's net worth is largely unaffected. Let's take an example, neglecting some of the niceties of taxes and convexities (changes in the effective duration) for the moment.

Suppose the investor buys a 4 percent, five-year, tax-exempt municipal bond to fund some of the investor's retirement in five years. Next, interest rates increase 1 percent. The price falls from 100 to about 96. The investor could sell and realize a capital loss, but since the bond will mature in five years, the better strategy is usually just to wait. Assuming that the investment and the liability are duration-matched, the increase in interest rates left the investor with approximately a net zero change in wealth. No matter what interest rates do, barring a default, the bond price at maturity will be par.

GETTING THE CHEAPEST DURATION

The general approach here is to identify a horizon and a liability. Once that is done, an individual bond or a portfolio with approximately the same duration as the liability is assembled. The asset portfolio should, of course, be the cheapest one available.

Barbells are a common method for finding the cheapest way to achieve a particular duration. Here a short- and a long-term bond are added to a portfolio. Duration-equivalent barbells are useful tools for investors. The duration of the barbell is a market value–weighted average of the individual durations of each bond. The return expected on the barbell can be compared with the return expected on an individual bond with the same duration. The barbell is often cheaper than the bond.

Using durations is not entirely passive. The duration of the assets and liabilities may drift over time and require periodic rebalancing. The frequency of rebalancing is a function of cost and complexity; it is typically done quarterly or annually.

INVESTING FOR WEALTH

Many investors buy for wealth preservation or wealth maximization and do not explicitly define a horizon. For most, the rule is to take what the market gives. Unless an investor is a credit expert, she should follow the ratings or other credit evaluations. In addition, the investor should make sure that the financials are regularly reported in EMMA. At all times, the investor should stay within her comfort zone in terms of credit and interest-rate exposure. Buying new issues during the retail order period can also be a good strategy to minimize costs.

PORTFOLIO CONSTRUCTION

An investor has a variety of options in constructing a portfolio. The most basic one is whether to own bonds directly or to buy a fund. Controlling the bonds directly allows the investor much more freedom of choice. For example, if the market trades off, a fund manager may be forced to sell bonds and realize a loss to meet redemptions, whereas an individual may well want to wait for the bond to mature at par. Most fund managers are good tax managers and try to avoid passing on losses to investors, but the market may not give them much latitude. On the other hand, the investor needs to have a large enough portfolio to hold at least 20 different issues in order to have an adequately diversified portfolio, so the investor may need to use a fund.

If the investor cannot diversify the portfolio with individual bonds, there are maturity-specific mutual funds and exchange-traded funds (ETFs) to choose among. Choosing between an ETF and a mutual fund may involve choosing between different investment styles. The typical mutual fund manager will actively manage the portfolio in order to maximize the return. While the fund shares are traded at the net asset value (NAV), the market value of the fund per share, the fund will have a variety of fees. The lowest-fee fund is not always the best choice, however, because the quality and experience of the manager can have a large effect on fund returns.

ETFs offer variety as well. They typically employ a passive investment style, tracking an index. Tracking a bond index can be a considerable challenge. The difference between the return on the ETF and the return on the fund is the tracking error. Investors need to be sure that the tracking error is small. ETF management fees are typically about 10 bp, lower than those of most mutual funds, but the shares of an ETF require paying a commission on each trade, and this may quickly add up for active traders.

An individual can employ a very straightforward passive investment strategy: a laddered portfolio. In a laddered portfolio, the investor buys an equal amount of par bonds along the yield curve. The ladder may be $5,000 invested every 2 years out to 10 years. This is a form of "buying the curve" that will benefit from an automatic liquidity feature, as the shortest bond matures every two years. The bonds will tend to appreciate as they roll down the steep front end of the municipal bond yield curve as well. Because the municipal yield curve is steeply rising, if yields remain the same, the ladder has intermediate yield risk, since the laddered portfolio has a duration equal to the average duration of the bonds in the ladder.

14

Derivatives

A derivative, as the name implies, is a security whose value is dependent on the price of another security. The security that determines the derivative's value is often referred to as the *underlying*. Internationally, the derivatives market is enormous and worthy of many volumes in and of itself. The derivatives market in municipals is not enormous; however, it has played a role that is disproportionate to its size.

The first part of this chapter is devoted to describing the wider derivatives market. In particular, we will devote some time to the more basic elements of fixed/floating London Interbank Offered Rate (LIBOR) interest-rate swaps. Following that, we will treat municipal bond–specific instruments.

THE BIG PICTURE

It is no longer possible to provide even a very complete synopsis of the international derivatives market with any brevity. Derivatives and derivatives based on underlyings that are themselves derivatives abound in all major currencies around the world. Most are currently OTC instruments, but that is likely to change as the Dodd-Frank rules come into play.

The derivatives markets had humble beginnings, from clay tablet contracts in 1750 BC Mesopotamia to 1849 futures contracts on the Chicago Board of Trade. Today it is the Bank for International Settlements (BIS) that keeps track of the scope of the international derivatives markets.

The nomenclature for derivatives is different from that for bonds, so a little preliminary work is necessary to understand the BIS data. Many of the derivatives we will deal with don't have face values. That is, when the derivative matures, the investor does not receive a lump sum the way he would with bonds. Instead, the size of the derivatives contract is described by its notional value.

The *notional value* is the amount that gets multiplied by an interest rate to determine interest payments. It generally functions like the face value of a bond, which, when multiplied by the coupon rate, gives the periodic interest payments to the bondholder; however, in interest-rate swaps, the notional amount is not paid as a cash payment in most cases.

The buyer and seller of a derivative are *counterparties*, not the usual issuer and investor. The counterparty that creates a derivative is the writer rather than the issuer. There are many other special terms in derivatives as well, and we will describe the more important ones as we confront them.

**Table 14-1   Global OTC Derivatives Market, 2010,
Amounts Outstanding (trillions of dollars)**

	Notional	Gross Market Value
Grand total	601,048	21,148
Interest-rate contracts	465,260	14,608
FRAs	51,587	206
Swaps	364,378	13,001
Options	49,295	1,401
Memo: Exchange-traded contracts	61,943	

Source: BIS.

The BIS reports on many types of derivatives, including equity and foreign exchange. The total notional amounts of OTC derivatives outstanding hit $601 trillion at the end of 2010. Worldwide credit exposure was $3.3 trillion. The exposure is less than the notional amount because the majority of the derivatives have risks offsetting another derivative's risk.

As Table 14-1 shows, by far the largest category of derivatives was interest-rate contracts with $465 trillion.

Interest-rate contracts traded on organized exchanges, while still large, amounted to only $62 trillion. Interest-rate swaps was an enormous category at $364 trillion, and its size is one reason we will examine it in some detail.

INTEREST-RATE SWAPS

The basic interest-rate swap is a fixed/floating agreement between two legal parties, the counterparties. The swap market is a high-grade institutional market, and the swaps are

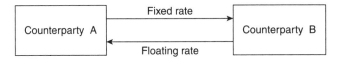

Figure 14-1   Plain Vanilla Swap

not rated. If one party is a lower-quality entity, it may be required to post collateral as security on the swap.

In a fixed/floating swap, one counterparty agrees to pay a fixed rate of interest to the other counterparty for the term of the agreement. The other counterparty pays a periodic floating-rate payment in return. Figure 14-1 shows an example of this type of plain vanilla fixed/floating swap.

Counterparty A is the payer of the fixed rate, and Counterparty B is the receiver of the fixed rate. Either or both of the counterparties may be dealers who make a market in derivatives. If the counterparty is not a dealer, it is a customer who adds the derivative to its portfolio.

The swap is typically documented with a short agreement that incorporates by reference a lengthy master agreement. The basis of the master agreement is usually provided by the International Swaps and Derivatives Association (ISDA), which is a global trade association for swap dealers.

Fixed/floating swaps are often defined by the nature of the floating rate. In municipal swaps, the seven-day Securities Industry and Financial Markets Association (SIFMA) swap rate that was discussed in the section on variable-rate demand obligations (VRDOs) is used as the floating leg of the swap, and so the swap is a SIFMA swap. Much more commonly, however, the floating rate is LIBOR. LIBOR is so important to the market that it is described in detail at the end of the chapter.

LIBOR swap rates have historically been much higher than SIFMA rates. As a result, issuers have chosen to pay a percentage of the LIBOR swap rate to reduce costs. For example, rather than pay the seven-day SIFMA rate, an issuer might choose to pay 67 percent of three-month LIBOR and receive that fraction of the LIBOR fixed swap rate.

LIBOR postings have been the subject of considerable controversy. As a result of the issues surrounding LIBOR, an alternative short-term rate is in use, the overnight index rate. The swaps using this are thus named overnight index swaps (OISs). In the United States, the floating side is a short-term rate, the fed funds rate. This is an unsecured interbank rate and is usually compounded daily.

When fixed/floating swaps are created, the present values of the floating and fixed sides are set to be equal. This is a par swap, and it has a value of zero, since the fixed side of the swap is set to market and the present values of the fixed and floating legs are equal. After it is created, the value of the swap can be greater or less than zero depending on the movement of interest rates. Swaps have durations similar to bonds.

Uses of Swaps

Fixed/floating swaps have a wide variety of uses. For investors, the swap is an asset that can be used to hedge interest rates, since being a fixed payer on a swap is effectively being short a bond. Suppose the investor has a 10-year bond. Its

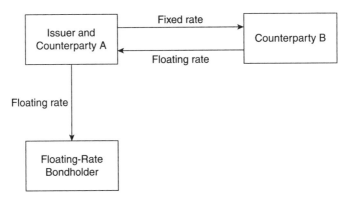

Figure 14-2   Synthetic Fixed-Rate Bond

interest-rate risk can be offset by being a payer on a 10-year swap. The hedge is more or less perfect depending on market conditions.

For issuers, swaps offer the ability to change the character of their debt from floating to fixed rate. Figure 14-2 shows a situation in which the issuer of a floating-rate bond enters into a swap contract with a Counterparty B. The payments are typically made quarterly on the floating side and semiannually on the fixed side. The payments are paid in arrears, that is, at the end of the period.

The issuer contracts to be a fixed payer on a swap and a receiver of a floating rate.

The floating rate is passed through to the bondholder. The net result is that the issuer has synthetically created a fixed-rate bond. The floating rate paid by the issuer may be tax-exempt, while the fixed rate received on the swap is taxable, since the swap could be embedded in the bond contract when issued. This would make it part of the issuer's bond transaction.

Rate Locks

Another application of the fixed/floating swap is the rate lock. This is similar to rate locks in mortgages. There the borrower can lock in the mortgage rate on a loan that will be closed in the future.

In the municipal market, the rate lock is used by issuers who want to lock in the current borrowing rate on a new bond issue that will be sold in the future. A rate lock employs a forward swap. In the fixed/floating swaps discussed thus far, the interest cash flows begin to accrue immediately. Just as with bonds, however, the swap does not have to be done in the spot market. The sale can be forward. In a forward transaction, the cash flows begin to accrue at some time in the future. For example, a bond can be sold one month forward. In that case, the bond will settle and the interest will begin to accrue a month after the sale date. The same notion applies to a fixed/floating swap. The cash flows can accrue forward rather than spot.

The forward swap can be combined with a new bond issue. Suppose the issuer wants to sell a new issue in a month, but would like to lock in today's fixed rate. One way to do that is to sell a fixed/floating swap one month forward. The issuer would be a fixed-rate payer and a floating-rate receiver. This commits the issuer to pay today's fixed rate. When a month passes, the issuer sells a floating-rate bond. The forward swap becomes current, and the issuer receives a floating rate on the swap, which it passes through to the bondholders on the new floating-rate issue. The issuer then begins to pay the fixed rate on the swap. In this way, the issuer has locked in the fixed rate.

MUNICIPAL BOND FUTURES

The desire to find an efficient way to short municipal bonds led to two attempts to develop a functional municipal futures contract. The first contract was devised in 1985 and received widespread industry support. Its design recognized that the contract could not depend on physical delivery of bonds because bonds in the municipal market were too thinly traded. The contract was based on a new index created for it, the Bond Buyer 40, which consisted of 40 "actively traded" bonds and was cash settled.

Alleged manipulation of the index led to the demise of this muni futures contract. A new muni futures contract was devised in 2002 based on a broader index, but it too failed. This time, the widespread use of LIBOR and SIFMA swaps contributed to thin trading in municipal futures. Structural problems also existed with the contract. At this point, the industry is awaiting a new and better design.

MUNI CDSs

Credit default swaps (CDSs) are also swaps. Here the payment between the counterparties is not based on an exchange of interest rates. Instead, one party sells credit insurance to the counterparty. The protection buyer pays the protection seller for the right to be compensated in the event that a bond or part of an index of bonds defaults. Like interest-rate swaps, CDSs usually pay on a quarterly basis. Municipal bond CDSs have two events of default: nonpayment and restructuring. Bankruptcy is not a condition of default.

The compensation for a default is the difference between the market value of the defaulted bond and par. If a default occurs, the protection seller buys the reference bond at par from the protection buyer. Presumably the bond is now selling at a substantial discount from par because the bond is in default. The protection seller can sell the bond in the secondary market and take the loss or hold the bond and hope that its value will improve in a workout with the issuer.

The ISDA Determinations Committee for the Americas region decides whether a default has occurred. The market price of the defaulted bond is established by a mandatory auction settlement. In a default, the bondholders are assumed to recover 75 percent of the face value of the bonds in a muni CDS contract.

The muni CDS market is a thinly traded institutional market. CDS contracts are traded on single names, like the states of New York and California. In addition, there are CDSs on indexes of municipal bonds. The most popular is the Markit MCDX. This consists of 50 different general obligation and revenue municipal bonds. The bonds have long maturities, but the CDS contracts are only for 3, 5, and 10 years.

THE BASICS OF LIBOR

LIBOR is the London Interbank Offered Rate. The rate is "fixed" or set once a day by the British Bankers' Association (BBA). The BBA rate, bbalibor™, is among the most important interest rates in the world. LIBOR is a bank lending rate, and the BBA says that the rate answers the following question:

At what rate could you borrow funds, were you to do so by asking for and then accepting inter-bank offers in a reasonable market size just prior to 11 am?

Some of the largest banks in the world are asked to provide indications of what their borrowing rates on loans that are not secured by assets or other deposits are likely to be. In other words, at what rate do these banks expect to be borrowing based on their own credit alone? The loans are expected to be large and of different currencies and maturities. Since these are the largest and typically most secure banks, LIBOR is expected to be the lowest or base rate.

LIBOR is quoted in 10 currencies and 15 different maturities, with overnight being the shortest and the others going out to a year. The bank intermarket for loans trades without regard to the official LIBOR rate; nevertheless, LIBOR-based bonds and derivatives mark to it, that is, the payments are based on the LIBOR rate. Every day a panel of banks is polled on their LIBOR rates. The top and bottom quarter are deleted and the others are averaged, giving the official postings.

The BBA lists the 20 banks that set the fixing of U.S. dollar bbalibor on November 2010:

- Bank of America
- Bank of Nova Scotia
- Bank of Tokyo-Mitsubishi UFJ Ltd
- Barclays Bank plc
- BNP Paribas

- Citibank NA
- Credit Agricole CIB
- Credit Suisse
- Deutsche Bank AG
- HSBC
- JPMorgan Chase
- Lloyds Banking Group
- Rabobank
- Royal Bank of Canada
- Société Générale
- Sumitomo Mitsui Banking Corporation
- The Norinchukin Bank
- The Royal Bank of Scotland Group
- UBS AG
- West LB AG

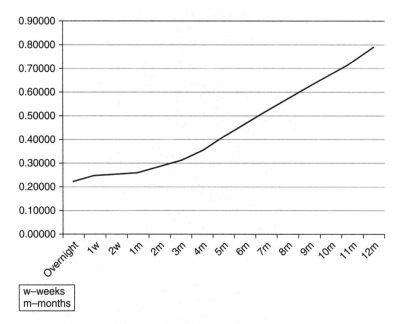

w—weeks
m—months

Figure 14-3   LIBOR Fixings, U.S. Dollar, Percent by Term, March 1, 2011 (*Source:* BBA.)

Officially the quotes are given on or about 11:00 a.m. London time. LIBOR rates are money market rates and are quoted on an annualized basis, so that even if the quote is for an overnight, the percent listed is as though it were repeated daily for a year. Figure 14-3 shows a sample of the fixings for U.S. dollar LIBOR on March 1, 2011.

15

The Checklist

The Financial Industry Regulatory Authority (FINRA) gives a list to help investors select bonds. I present it here as a bit of a review for the book.

MUNI BOND CHECKLIST

Use this checklist to help avoid some of the most common pitfalls of municipal bond investing.

❑ *Verify the type of bond (general obligation vs. revenue), and make sure you understand the bond's terms and risk factors.*

❑ *Ask to see—and read or have your broker review with you— the bond's Official Statement before you purchase a bond, particularly if it is a new issue. The Official Statement will be a valuable tool for understanding the terms of any bond you might buy in the secondary market, but be aware that the financial and operating data may have been superseded by the issuer's on-going disclosures.*

❑ *Confirm with your broker whether the issuer is current in its disclosure filings and be sure to review the information in the on-going disclosures. Be wary of bonds whose issuers are not current in their disclosure filings.*

❑ *Keep tabs on your bond's credit rating and the issuer's creditworthiness. Has the issuer of the bond recently been downgraded? Has the issuer filed any default or other material event notices?*

❑ *If the bond is insured or otherwise backed by a third-party, verify the credit rating of the bond insurer or other backing.*

❑ *If you buy a bond in the secondary market, be sure to ask why the bond is priced as it is. Be aware that the price of a bond can be priced above or below its par value for many reasons, including changes in the creditworthiness of a bond's issuer and a host of other factors, including prevailing interest rates.*

❑ *Understand how the bond's interest will be paid. Most muni bonds pay semiannually, but zero coupon municipal bonds pay all interest at the time the bond matures and the principal is returned. Variable rate bonds typically will pay interest more frequently, usually on a monthly basis in variable amounts.*

❑ *Understand the bond's tax implications, including the possibility that your bond may be subject to the federal Alternative Minimum Tax (AMT) or may be fully taxable. Also understand whether the bond enjoys any state tax benefits. Consider consulting a tax professional before buying a muni.*

❑ *Know a bond's call provisions. Call provisions allow the issuer to retire the bond before it matures. You can find the call provisions in the Official Statement.*

❑ *Know what you are paying for your bond, which will be reported on your confirmation statement. Most bonds are sold without a commission—instead, the broker usually is compensated through a dealer's spread, or profit, which is included within the price. If a commission is charged, this will also be reported on your confirmation statement.*

❑ *Review your confirmation statement to be sure the information is accurate and in line with what you were told by your broker and contained in the Official Statement.*

Glossary of Acronyms

ACE	adjusted current earnings
AGC	Assured Guaranty Corp.
AGI	adjusted gross income
AGM	Assured Guaranty Municipal bond insurance
AMBAC	American Municipal Bond Assurance Corporation
AMT	Alternative Minimum Tax
AMTI	Alternative Minimum Taxable Income
AON	all-or-none
ARRA	American Recovery and Reinvestment Act of 2009
B	broker's broker trade
BABs	Build America Bonds
BBA	British Bankers' Association
BIS	Bank for International Settlements
bp	basis point
CAB	compound accretion bond
CAPM	capital asset pricing model
CDO	collateralized debt obligation
CDS	credit default swaps
CREB	clean renewable energy bond
CUSIP	Committee on Uniform Securities Identification Procedures
EMMA	MSRB's Electronic Municipal Market Access
EOP	extraordinary optional call

ETF	exchange-traded fund
ETM	escrowed to maturity bond
FGIC	Financial Guaranty Insurance Company
FINRA	Financial Industry Regulatory Authority
FSA	Financial Security Assurance, Inc.
GAO	U.S. Government Accountability Office
GASB	Government Accounting Standards Board
GDP	Gross Domestic Product
GO	general obligation bond
ISDA	International Swaps and Derivatives Association
L	list offering price
LADWP	Los Angeles Department of Water and Power
LIBOR	London Interbank Offered Rate
LO	legal opinion
LOC	letter of credit
MBIA	Municipal Bond Insurance Association
MMD	Municipal Market Data
MSRB	Municipal Securities Rulemaking Board
NAV	net asset value
NIC	net interest cost
NRSRO	nationally recognized statistical rating organization
OID	original issue discount
OIP	original issue premium
OIS	overnight index swap

OPEBs	other postemployment benefits
OS	official statement
OTC	over-the-counter
P	weighted-average price trade
P&C	property and casualty insurance company
POS	preliminary official statement
QECB	qualified energy conservation bond
QSCB	qualified school construction bond
QZAB	qualified zone academy bond
RZEDB	recovery zone economic development bond
SBPA	standby bonds purchase agreement
SEC	Securities and Exchange Commission
SIFMA	Securities Industry and Financial Markets Association
SLG	State and Local Government
SMMP	sophisticated municipal market professional
TAF	Term Auction Facility
TIC	true interest cost
TOB	tender option bond
VRDO	variable rate demand obligation
W	when-issued trade
WD	withdrawn
WPPSS	Washington Public Power Supply System

Note: For a definition of terms used in this book, please see http://www.investinginbonds.com/story.asp?id=3140

References

CHAPTER 1: A LITTLE HISTORY

Books and Articles

Dewey, Davis Rich. *Early Financial History of the United States*. 12th ed. Washington, DC: Beard Books, 1934.

Spiotto, James E. "Historical and Legal Strength of State and Local Government Debt Financing: In Good Times and Bad Times; Financial Challenges Past, Present and Future." Webinar. November 2010. http://www.chapman.com/events/20101116/SpiottoWebinar _111610.pdf.

Lowenstein, Roger. "Broke Town, U.S.A." *New York Times*. March 3, 2011. http://www.nytimes.com/2011/03/06/magazine/06Muni-t.html? pagewanted=all#h[BtfAtr,3].

Han, Song, and Dan Li. "Liquidity Crisis, Runs, and Security Design." Social Science Research Network. February 15, 2009. http://papers .ssrn.com/soL3/papers.cfm?abstract_id=1344136.

Websites Consulted

Federal Reserve Bank of San Francisco. "Colonial and Continental Currency: Notes of the Original 13 Colonies." Accessed June 18, 2012. http://www.frbsf.org/currency/independence/original/s06.html.

U.S. Constitution online. "The U.S. Constitution, Article 1, Section 8." Last modified August 16, 2010. http://www.usconstitution.net /xconst_A1Sec8.html.

U.S. Constitution online. "The U.S. Constitution, Article 1, Section 10." Last modified January 24, 2010. http://www.usconstitution.net /xconst_A1Sec10.html.

U.S. Constitution online. "The U.S. Constitution, Article 6." Last modified January 24, 2010. http://www.usconstitution.net/xconst _A6.html.

U.S. Constitution online. "The U.S. Constitution, Amendment 5." Last modified January 24, 2010. http://www.usconstitution.net/xconst _Am5.html.

FindLaw. "*Edwards v. People of State of California*, 314 U.S. 160 (1941)." Accessed June 18, 2012. http://caselaw.lp.findlaw.com/scripts /getcase.pl?navby=search&court=US&case=/us/314/160.html.

Moody's.com. "Moody's Investors Service—Special Comment: U.S. Municipal Bond Defaults and Recoveries, 1970–2011." March 7, 2012. http://www.moodys.com/researchdocumentcontentpage.aspx? docid=PBC_140114.

aps.edu. "Official Statement Dated April 20, 2011—$27,540,000— Albuquerque Municipal School District No. 12." Accessed June 18, 2012. http://www.aps.edu/finance/accounting/bonds/Official% 20Statement%2004-20-2011.pdf.

The website of Exploring Constitutional Law. "The Supremacy Clause and Federal Preemption." Accessed June 20, 2012. http://law2 .umkc.edu/faculty/projects/ftrials/conlaw/preemption.htm.

HG.org. "Bankruptcy Law." Accessed June 18, 2012. http://www.hg.org /bankrpt.html.

U.S. Constitution online. "The U.S. Constitution, Amendment 10." Last modified January 24, 2010. http://www.usconstitution.net/xconst _Am10.html.

www.mintz.com. "Bankruptcy and Public Finance Advisory: Bankruptcy Judge Rules That City of Vallejo Can Void Union Contracts." Mintz Levin Publications. April 15, 2009. http://www.mintz.com /publications/1804/Bankruptcy_and_Public_Finance_Advisory _Bankruptcy_Judge_Rules_that_City_of_Vallejo_Can_Void _Union_Contracts.

The website of Allegheny Institute for Public Policy. "Municipal Bankcruptcy: Issue Summary." Updated January 2011. http:// alleghenyinstitute.org/government/munbankruptcy.html.

Flickr.com. "Ford to City: Drop Dead." *New York Daily News* headline (1975). Accessed June 20, 2012. http://www.flickr.com/photos /untergeek/17881729/.

The website of the Federal Reserve Bank of St. Louis. "The Financial Crisis: A Timeline of Events and Policy Actions." Accessed June 18, 2012. http://timeline.stlouisfed.org/index.cfm?p=timeline.

The website of the Association of Financial Guaranty Insurers. "Who We Are." Accessed June 18, 2012. http://www.afgi.org/whoweare.htm.

Legal Citations

United States Trust Company of New York v. New Jersey, 431 U.S. 1 (1977).

Revised Municipal Bankruptcy Act in 1937, Pub. L. No. 302, 50 Stat. 653 (1937).

11 U.S.C. 101(40).

11 U.S.C. 109(c)(2).

11 U.S.C. 109(c)(5).

In re City of Vallejo, Case No. 08-26813-A-9 (Bankr. E.D. Cal. March 13, 2009).

Charts, Tables, and Pictures

Shenai, Siddharth Bhaskar, et al. "Financial Guarantors and the 2007–2009 Credit Crisis." AFA 2011 Denver Meetings Paper. March 15, 2010. Table 4, p. 38. http://dx.doi.org/10.2139/ssrn.1571627.

The website of the U.S. Census Bureau. "State and Local Government Finances and Employment: Governmental Units—428—Number of Governmental Units, by Type." *Statistical Abstract of the United States, 2012*. Accessed June 18, 2012. http://www.census.gov/compendia/statab/cats/state_local_govt_finances_employment/governmental_units.html.

CHAPTER 2: A FIRST LOOK AT MUNICIPAL BONDS

Books and Articles

Biais, Bruno, and Richard C. Green. "The Microstructure of the Bond Market in the 20th Century." Toulouse University and

Carnegie Mellon University Working Paper. August 29, 2007. http://wpweb2.tepper.cmu.edu/facultyadmin/upload/wpaper _39493927532128_biasgreen8-29.pdf.

Harris, Lawrence E., and Michael S. Piwowar. "Secondary Trading Costs in the Municipal Bond Market." *Journal of Finance* 61, no. 3 (June 2006): 1361–1397. DOI: 10.1111/j.1540-6261.2006.00875.x.

Green, Richard C., et al. "Price Discovery in Illiquid Markets: Do Financial Asset Prices Rise Faster than They Fall?" Columbia.edu. April 2, 2009. http://www4.gsb.columbia.edu/filemgr?file_id=7316.

Websites Consulted

The website of the Municipal Securities Rulemaking Board. Accessed June 18, 2012. http://msrb.org/.

The website of the Financial Industry Regulatory Authority. "About the Financial Industry Regulatory Authority." Accessed June 18, 2012. http://www.finra.org/AboutFINRA/index.htm.

The website of the Municipal Securities Rulemaking Board. "Anti-Fraud Provisions." Accessed June 18, 2012. http://www.msrb.org/msrb1 /glossary/view_def.asp?param=ANTIFRAUDPROVISIONS.

The website of Nixon Peabody LLP. "New MSRB Rule G-17 Interpretive Notice to Require Underwriters to Make New Disclosures to Issuers." *Public Finance Alert*. May 25, 2012. http://www.nixonpeabody.com /publications_detail3.asp?ID=4431.

The website of the Municipal Securities Rulemaking Board. "Rule G-17— Conduct of Municipal Securities and Municipal Advisory Activities— Interpretive Notices." Accessed June 20, 2012. http://www.msrb .org/Rules-and-Interpretations/MSRB-Rules/General/Rule-G-17 .aspx?tab=2#_D37D3EF9-F642-4A63-A40D-3A6B33B5260A.

The website of Electronic Municipal Market Access. Accessed June 18, 2012. http://emma.msrb.org/.

www.sec.gov. "Re: Comments on Volcker Rule Proposed Regulations." SIFMA correspondence. February 13, 2012. http://www.sec.gov /comments/s7-41-11/s74111-202.pdf.

www.irs.gov. "Publication 970 (2011), Tax Benefits for Education." Accessed June 20, 2012. http://www.irs.gov/publications/p970 /ch08.html#en_US_2011_publink1000178531.

The website of CUSIP Global Services. Accessed June 18, 2012. https:// www.cusip.com/cusip/index.htm.

Charts, Tables, and Pictures

The website of the U.S. Government Accountability Office. "Municipal Securities: Overview of Market Structure, Pricing and Regulation." January 2012. http://www.gao.gov/assets/590/587714.pdf.

The website of Electronic Municipal Market Access. "Market Activity." Accessed May 31, 2012. http://emma.msrb.org/.

The website of the Municipal Securities Rulemaking Board. "Accrued Interest." Accessed June 18, 2012. http://www.msrb.org/msrb1 /glossary/view_def.asp?param=ACCRUEDINTEREST.

"Bloomberg PICK Screen—All Offerings." Bloomberg Terminal. Accessed June 18, 2012.

"Bloomberg MBWD Screen—Investors Offering Bonds." Bloomberg Terminal. Accessed June 18, 2012.

"Bloomberg MBWD Screen—Bid Wanted." Bloomberg Terminal. Accessed June 18, 2012.

CHAPTER 3: READING AN OFFICIAL STATEMENT

Books and Articles

Bierwag, G. O. "Optimal TIC Bids on Serial Bond Issues." *Management Science* 22, no. 11 (July 1976): 1175–1185. DOI: 10.1287/mnsc .22.11.1175.

Websites Consulted

www.investinginbonds.com by SIFMA. "Glossary of Bond Terms." Accessed June 18, 2012. http://www.investinginbonds.com/story .asp?id=3140.

Legal Citations

IRC Section 103.

Charts, Tables, and Pictures

The website of Electronic Municipal Market Access. "Security Details—State of Illinois Official Statement." Accessed June 18, 2012. http://emma.msrb.org/SecurityView/SecurityDetails.aspx?cusip=A0753A7668CBE067D397A1008DB7BDD4E.

CHAPTER 4: A REVENUE BOND EXAMPLE

Books and Articles

Depaul, Jennifer. "Private Activity Bond Cap to Increase in 2012." *The Bond Buyer*, December 23, 2011. http://www.bondbuyer.com/issues/120_247/private-activity-bond-cap-1034597-1.html.

Internal Revenue Bulletin, No. 2012-13, March 26, 2012. http://www.irs.gov/pub/irs-irbs/irb12-13.pdf.

Gonze, Josh. "The Alternative Minimum Tax and Municipal Bond Fund Investing." *Thornburg Articles*. Accessed June 20, 2012. http://www.thornburginvestments.com/research/articles/AMT.asp.

Johnson, Anastasija. "Calif Calls for Reform of 'Unfair' Muni Ratings." Reuters. March 3, 2008. http://www.reuters.com/article/2008/03/03/us-municipals-ratings-idUSN0336806020080303.

Seymour, Dan. "Fitch Will Revise Its Municipal Credit Ratings in April." *The Bond Buyer*, March 25, 2010. http://www.bondbuyer.com/news/fitch_revise_credit_rating-1010065-1.html.

Hempel, George H. "Past Payment Performance." *The Postwar Quality of State and Local Debt*. Cambridge, MA: National Bureau of Economic Research, 1971. Accessed June 18, 2012. http://www.nber.org/chapters/c3427.pdf.

Websites Consulted

ca.gov. "State Administrative Manual: General Obligation (GO) Bonds."
Last updated July 10, 2007. http://sam.dgs.ca.gov/TOC/6000
/6871.htm.

The website of Davis Polk & Wardwell LLP. "Summary of the Dodd-
Frank Wall Street Reform and Consumer Protection Act, Enacted
into Law on July 21, 2010." July 21, 2010. http://www.davispolk
.com/files/Publication/7084f9fe-6580-413b-b870-b7c025ed2ecf
/Presentation/PublicationAttachment/1d4495c7-0be0-4e9a-ba77
-f786fb90464a/070910_Financial_Reform_Summary.pdf.

Legal Citations

Rev. Rul. 63-20, 1963-1 C.B. 24.
Rev. Proc. 82-26, 1982-1 C.B. 114.

Charts, Tables, and Pictures

The website of Electronic Municipal Market Access. "City of Los
Angeles Official Statement." Accessed June 18, 2012. http://emma
.msrb.org/MS278489-MS276912-MD561824.pdf.

Washburn, Lisa. "Moody's US Municipal Bond Rating Scale." Special
Comment. November 2002. http://www.moodys.com/sites
/products/defaultresearch/2001700000407258.pdf.

www.fitchratings.com. "Fitch Ratings U.S. Public Finance 2011
Transition and Default Study." Special Report. March 12, 2012.

CHAPTER 5: CONDUIT FINANCING

Charts, Tables, and Pictures

The website of Electronic Municipal Market Access. "Arizona Health
Facilities Official Statement." Accessed June 18, 2012. http://emma

.msrb.org/OSPreview/OSPreview.aspx?documentId=MS266296&
transactionId=MS270059&fileId=MD521774.

CHAPTER 6: REFUNDINGS

Books and Articles

Seymour, Dan. "Fitch Will Revise Its Municipal Credit Ratings in
April." *The Bond Buyer*, March 25, 2010. http://www.bondbuyer
.com/news/fitch_revise_credit_rating-1010065-1.html.

Websites Consulted

www.irs.gov. "Module E—Refunding." Accessed June 18, 2012. http://
www.irs.gov/pub/irs-tege/trng_phaseiie.pdf.
TreasuryDirect. "SLGS FAQ." Last updated April 12, 2012. https://
www.treasurydirect.gov/govt/resources/faq/faq_slgs.htm.

Legal Citations

Treas. Reg. Section 1.150-1(d)(1).

Charts, Tables, and Pictures

sifma.org. "Statistics—Municipal—US Municipal Issuance (xls)."
Accessed July 25, 2012. http://www.sifma.org/research/statistics
.aspx.
The website of Electronic Municipal Market Access. "Escrow Deposit
Agreement Between Heartland Consumers Power District and
The First National Bank in Sioux Falls, as Escrow Agent." Dated
as of June 1, 2011. http://emma.msrb.org/ER483591-ER376168
-ER774168.pdf.

CHAPTER 7: ELEMENTS OF TAXATION

Books and Articles

Ang, Andrew, et al. "Taxes on Tax-Exempt Bonds." Social Science Research Network. November 11, 2008. http://papers.ssrn.com /sol3/papers.cfm?abstract_id=1946499.

Erickson, Merle M., et al. "How Prevalent Is Tax Arbitrage? Evidence from the Market for Municipal Bonds." *National Tax Journal* 56, no. 1 (March 2003): 259.

Joint Committee on Taxation. "Background Information on Tax Expenditure Analysis and Historical Survey of Tax Expenditure Estimates." March 9, 2011. https://www.jct.gov/publications .html?func=startdown&id=3740.

Websites Consulted

ucf.edu. "TAX 6845: Tax Planning and Consulting—Topic: Alternative Minimum Tax." Last updated October 11, 2010. http://www .bus.ucf.edu/faculty/ckelliher/file.axd?file=2011/1/alternative _minimum_tax_notes.pdf.

H&RBlock.com. "Tax Tips & Calculators." Accessed June 18, 2012. http://www.hrblock.com/taxes/tax_tips/tax_planning/amt.html.

The website of State Tax Central. "Multistate: Individual Taxes: Alternative Minimum Tax: State Taxes." Accessed June 18, 2012. http://www.statetaxcentral.com/Multistate/Individual_Taxes /Alternative_Minimum_Tax/.

Legal Citations

South Carolina v. Baker, 485 U.S. 505 (1988).

IRC Section 265(a).

Rev. Proc. 72-18.

Department of Revenue of Kentucky v. Davis, 553 U.S. 328 (2008).

Congressional Budget and Impoundment Control Act of 1974, Pub. L. No. 93-344, 88 Stat. 297 (1974).

CHAPTER 8: TAXABLE MUNICIPAL BONDS

Books and Articles

Bailey, Michael G., et al. "The American Recovery and Reinvestment Act of 2009: New Financing Tools for State and Local Governments—'Build America Bonds.'" Foley and Lardner LLP. February 18, 2009. http://www.foley.com/publications/pub_detail.aspx?pubid=5728.

Websites Consulted

TreasuryDirect. "IRS Tax Credit Bond Rates." Last updated October 19, 2009. https://www.treasurydirect.gov/govt/rates/rates_irstcb.htm.

Orrick.com. "Pension Obligation Bond Financing." Accessed June 18, 2012. http://www.orrick.com/practices/public_finance/pension.asp.

Charts, Tables, and Pictures

The website of *The Bond Buyer*. "A Decade of Municipal Bond Finance." Accessed May 16, 2012. http://www.bondbuyer.com/marketstatistics/decade_1/.

The website of Electronic Municipal Market Access. "Security Details—City of San Antonio Official Statement." Accessed June 18, 2012. http://emma.msrb.org/SecurityView/SecurityDetails.aspx?cusip=AFEBCCACB23ED20DFE89D5B1647193992.

CHAPTER 9: THE MICROSTRUCTURE OF THE MUNICIPAL BOND MARKET

Websites Consulted

The website of Foster Swift LLP. "Updates on Federal Tax Laws Affecting Municipal Bonds." January 2011. http://www.fosterswift.com/news-publications-Federal-Tax-Laws-Affecting-Municipal-Bonds.html.

sifma.org. "About the Municipal Swap Index." November 1, 2010. http://www.sifma.org/research/item.aspx?id=1690.

sifma.org. "Muni Swap Index Data." March 21, 2012. http://www.sifma.org/research/item.aspx?id=19762.

Charts, Tables, and Pictures

sifma.org. "Research—Statistics." Last updated August 3, 2012. http://www.sifma.org/research/statistics.aspx.

The website of the U.S. Census Bureau. "Income, Expenditures, Poverty, & Wealth: Gross Domestic Product." *Statistical Abstract of the United States, 2012.* Accessed June 18, 2012. http://www.census.gov/compendia/statab/cats/income_expenditures_poverty_wealth/gross_domestic_product_gdp.html.

The website of *The Bond Buyer*, "A Decade of Municipal Bond Finance." Accessed May 16, 2012. http://www.bondbuyer.com/marketstatistics/decade_1/.

Board of Governors of the Federal Reserve System. "Flow of Funds Accounts of the United States—Federal Reserve Statistical Release." U.S. Federal Reserve. June 7, 2012. Table L.211. http://www.federalreserve.gov/Releases/Z1/Current/z1.pdf.

www.irs.gov. "SOI Tax Stats—Individual Statistical Tables by Size of Adjusted Gross Income—Individual Complete Report." Publication 1304. Table 1.1. Page last reviewed or updated June 6, 2012. http://www.irs.gov/taxstats/indtaxstats/article/0,,id=96981,00.html.

CHAPTER 10: STATE AND LOCAL ECONOMIES

Books and Articles

The *Economist* Online. "Comparing US States with Countries: Stateside Substitutes." January 13, 2011. http://www.economist.com/blogs/dailychart/2011/01/comparing_us_states_countries.

James, Michael. "Working in America: Public vs. Private Sector." *ABC News Blogs—George Stephanopoulos.* February 18, 2011. http://blogs.abcnews.com/george/2011/02/working-in-america-public-vs-private-sector.html.

Websites Consulted

The website of the Bureau of Economic Analysis. "Widespread Economic Growth Across States in 2011." Last updated June 5, 2012. http://www.bea.gov/newsreleases/regional/gdp_state/gsp_newsrelease.htm.

Calpensions.com. "Moody Begins Treating Pensions like Bond Debt." June 27, 2011. http://calpensions.com/2011/01/31/moodys-begins-treating-pensions-like-bond-debt/.

Charts, Tables, and Pictures

Barnett, Jeffrey L. "State and Local Governments Finances Summary 2008." U.S. Census Bureau. April 2011. http://www2.census.gov/govs/estimate/08statesummaryreport.pdf.

The website of the U.S. Census Bureau. "State & Local Gov't Finances & Employment: Federal Aid to State and Local Governments." *Statistical Abstract of the United States, 2012.* Accessed June 18, 2012. http://www.census.gov/compendia/statab/cats/state_local_govt_finances_employment/federal_aid_to_state_and_local_governments.html.

The website of the U.S. Census Bureau. "State & Local Government Finance." Accessed June 18, 2012. http://www.census.gov/govs/estimate/.

CHAPTER 11: THE YIELD CURVE

Books and Articles

Avellaneda, Marco, and Jeong-Hyun Lee. "Statistical Arbitrage in the U.S. Equities Market." nyu.edu. July 11, 2008. http://www.math.nyu.edu/faculty/avellane/AvellanedaLeeStatArb071108.pdf.

Dwyer, Gerald P., and Paula Tkac. "The Financial Crisis of 2008 in Fixed Income Markets." Federal Reserve Bank of Atlanta Working Paper Series. August 1, 2009. http://papers.ssrn.com/sol3/papers.cfm?abstract_id=1464891.

Websites Consulted

www.sec.gov. "Re: Comments on Volcker Rule Proposed Regulations." SIFMA correspondence. February 13, 2012. http://www.sec.gov/comments/s7-41-11/s74111-202.pdf.

Charts, Tables, and Pictures

The website of Electronic Municipal Market Access. "Security Details— State of Illinois Official Statement." Accessed June 18, 2012. http://emma.msrb.org/SecurityView/SecurityDetails.aspx?cusip=A0753A7668CBE067D397A1008DB7BDD4E.

The website of Thomson Reuters. "The Municipal Market Monitor (TM3)." Accessed June 18, 2012. https://www.tm3.com/homepage/homepage.jsf?ur=y.

federalreserve.gov. "Selected Interest Rates (Daily)—H.15—Historical Data." Accessed June 18, 2012. http://www.federalreserve.gov/releases/h15/data.htm.

The website of Electronic Municipal Market Access. "Market Statistics— Trade Summary & Charts—Trade Type Summary." Accessed June 18, 2012. http://emma.msrb.org/M/ViewStatistics.aspx.

CHAPTER 12: MUNICIPAL BOND YIELD CALCULATIONS

Books and Articles

Watkins, Thayer. "Irving Fisher's Theory of Interest Rates with or Without Adjustment for Tax Rates and Risk Premiums." San Jose

State University. Accessed June 18, 2012. http://www.sjsu.edu
/faculty/watkins/fisher1.htm.

Charts, Tables, and Pictures

"Bloomberg FTAX Calculator." Bloomberg Terminal. Accessed June 18,
    2012.
www.irs.gov. "Publication 17 (2011)—14. Sale of Property—Holding
    Period." Accessed June 18, 2012. http://www.irs.gov/publications
    /p17/ch14.html#en_US_2011_publink1000172339.
"Bloomberg YA Screen." Bloomberg Terminal. Accessed June 18, 2012.

CHAPTER 13: ELEMENTS OF PORTFOLIO STRUCTURING

Websites Consulted

The website of the Government Finance Officers Association. "Best Prac-
    tice: Analyzing and Issuing Refunding Bonds." February 2011. http://
    www.gfoa.org/index.php?option=com_content&task=view&
    id=1572.
www.irs.gov. "Tax Exempt Private Activity Bonds." Accessed June 18,
    2012. www.irs.gov/pub/irs-pdf/p4078.pdf.

CHAPTER 14: DERIVATIVES

Books and Articles

Dudney, Donna, and John Geppert. "Do Tax-Exempt Yields Adjust
    Slowly to Substantial Changes in Taxable Yields?" *Journal of Futures
    Markets* 28, no. 8 (2008): 763–789. DOI: 10.1002/fut.20332.

Websites Consulted

"Derivative Market Size." EconomyWatch. November 23, 2011. http://www.economywatch.com/market/derivative-market/size.html.

The website of BBA LIBOR, "BBA Libor—The Basics." Accessed June 18, 2012. http://www.bbalibor.com/bbalibor-explained/the-basics.

Charts, Tables, and Pictures

bis.org. "Semiannual OTC Derivatives Statistics at End-December 2011." June 2012. http://www.bis.org/statistics/derstats.htm.

The website of BBA LIBOR. "BBA Libor Panels." Accessed March 1, 2011. http://www.bbalibor.com/news-releases/bba-libor-panels7.

The website of BBA LIBOR, "Historical Libor Rates." Accessed March 1, 2011. http://www.bbalibor.com/rates/historical.

CHAPTER 15: THE CHECKLIST

Charts, Tables, and Pictures

The website of the Financial Industry Regulatory Authority. "Muni Bond Checklist." Accessed June 18, 2012. http://www.finra.org/Investors/ProtectYourself/InvestorAlerts/Bonds/p118925.

Bibliography

Ang, Andrew, et al. "Taxes on Tax-Exempt Bonds." Social Science Research Network. November 11, 2008. http://papers.ssrn.com /sol3/papers.cfm?abstract_id=1946499.

Avellaneda, Marco, and Jeong-Hyun Lee. "Statistical Arbitrage in the U.S. Equities Market." nyu.edu. July 11, 2008. http://www.math .nyu.edu/faculty/avellane/AvellanedaLeeStatArb071108.pdf.

Bailey, Michael G., et al. "The American Recovery and Reinvestment Act of 2009: New Financing Tools for State and Local Governments— 'Build America Bonds.'" Foley and Lardner LLP. February 18, 2009. http://www.foley.com/publications/pub_detail.aspx?pubid=5728.

Barnett, Jeffrey L. "State and Local Governments Finances Summary 2008." U.S. Census Bureau. April 2011. http://www2.census.gov /govs/estimate/08statesummaryreport.pdf.

Biais, Bruno, and Richard C. Green. "The Microstructure of the Bond Market in the 20th Century." Toulouse University and Carnegie Mellon University Working Paper. August 29, 2007. http://wpweb2 .tepper.cmu.edu/facultyadmin/upload/wpaper_39493927532128 _biasgreen8-29.pdf.

Bierwag, G. O. "Optimal TIC Bids on Serial Bond Issues." *Management Science* 22, no. 11 (July 1976): 1175–1185. DOI: 10.1287/mnsc .22.11.1175.

Depaul, Jennifer. "Private Activity Bond Cap to Increase in 2012." *The Bond Buyer*, December 23, 2011. http://www.bondbuyer.com /issues/120_247/private-activity-bond-cap-1034597-1.html.

Dewey, Davis Rich. *Early Financial History of the United States.* 12th ed. Washington, DC: Beard Books, 1934.

Dudney, Donna, and John Geppert. "Do Tax-Exempt Yields Adjust Slowly to Substantial Changes in Taxable Yields?" *Journal of Futures Markets* 28, no. 8 (2008): 763–789. DOI: 10.1002/fut.20332.

Dwyer, Gerald P., and Paula Tkac. "The Financial Crisis of 2008 in Fixed Income Markets." Federal Reserve Bank of Atlanta Working Paper Series. August 1, 2009. http://papers.ssrn.com/sol3/papers .cfm?abstract_id=1464891.

Erickson. Merle M., et al. "How Prevalent Is Tax Arbitrage? Evidence from the Market for Municipal Bonds." *National Tax Journal* 56, no. 1 (March 2003).

Feldstein, Sylvan G., and Frank J. Fabozzi, eds. *The Handbook of Municipal Bonds*. Hoboken, NJ: Wiley, 2008.

Gonze, Josh. "The Alternative Minimum Tax and Municipal Bond Fund Investing." *Thornburg Articles*. Accessed June 20, 2012. http:// www.thornburginvestments.com/research/articles/AMT.asp.

Green, Richard C., et al, "Price Discovery in Illiquid Markets: Do Financial Asset Prices Rise Faster than They Fall?" Columbia.edu. April 2, 2009. http://www4.gsb.columbia.edu/filemgr?file_id=7316.

Han, Song, and Dan Li. "Liquidity Crisis, Runs, and Security Design." Social Science Research Network. February 15, 2009. http://papers .ssrn.com/soL3/papers.cfm?abstract_id=1344136.

Harris, Lawrence E., and Michael S. Piwowar. "Secondary Trading Costs in the Municipal Bond Market." *Journal of Finance* 61, no. 3 (June 2006): 1361–1397. DOI: 10.1111/j.1540-6261.2006.00875.x.

Hempel, George H. "Past Payment Performance." *The Postwar Quality of State and Local Debt*. Cambridge, MA: National Bureau of Economic Research, 1971. Accessed June 18, 2012. http://www.nber.org /chapters/c3427.pdf.

Internal Revenue Bulletin, No. 2012-13, March 26, 2012. http://www.irs. gov/pub/irs-irbs/irb12-13.pdf.

James, Michael. "Working in America: Public vs. Private Sector." *ABC News Blogs—George Stephanopoulos*. February 18, 2011. http://blogs .abcnews.com/george/2011/02/working-in-america-public-vs- private-sector.html.

Johnson, Anastasija. "Calif Calls for Reform of 'Unfair' Muni Ratings." Reuters, March 3, 2008. http://www.reuters.com/article/2008/03 /03/us-municipals-ratings-idUSN0336806020080303.

Joint Committee on Taxation. "Background Information on Tax Expenditure Analysis and Historical Survey of Tax Expenditure Estimates." March 9, 2011. https://www.jct.gov/publications.html?func=startdown&id=3740.

Lowenstein, Roger. "Broke Town, U.S.A." *New York Times*, March 3, 2011. http://www.nytimes.com/2011/03/06/magazine/06Muni-t.html?pagewanted=all#h[BtfAtr,3].

Seymour, Dan. "Fitch Will Revise Its Municipal Credit Ratings in April." *The Bond Buyer*, March 25, 2010. http://www.bondbuyer.com/news/fitch_revise_credit_rating-1010065-1.html.

Shenai, Siddharth Bhaskar, et al. "Financial Guarantors and the 2007–2009 Credit Crisis." AFA 2011 Denver Meetings Paper. March 15, 2010. http://dx.doi.org/10.2139/ssrn.1571627.

Spiotto, James E. "Historical and Legal Strength of State and Local Government Debt Financing: In Good Times and Bad Times; Financial Challenges Past, Present and Future." Webinar. November 2010. http://www.chapman.com/events/20101116/SpiottoWebinar_111610.pdf.

The *Economist* Online. "Comparing US States with Countries: Stateside Substitutes." January 13, 2011. http://www.economist.com/blogs/dailychart/2011/01/comparing_us_states_countries.

Washburn, Lisa. "Moody's US Municipal Bond Rating Scale." Special Comment. November 2002. http://www.moodys.com/sites/products/defaultresearch/2001700000407258.pdf.

Watkins, Thayer. "Irving Fisher's Theory of Interest Rates with or Without Adjustment for Tax Rates and Risk Premiums." San Jose State University. Accessed June 18, 2012. http://www.sjsu.edu/faculty/watkins/fisher1.htm.

Index

About the Author

PHILIP FISCHER is the managing partner at eBooleant Consulting, LLC, a financial and computer consulting firm. He has appeared as a bond market expert on Bloomberg TV and radio and has been quoted by publications including: the *Wall Street Journal*, *Barron's*, the *New York Times*, *Financial Times*, and *Reuters*. He was the recipient of NFMA's 2003 Award of Excellence and the Municipal Bond Buyers Conference Certificate of Recognition for Outstanding Service in 2010. He has been identified as an all-star analyst for 10 years by Smith's Research and *Institutional Investor* magazine.

Formerly the head of Municipal Bond Research and the Global Index System for Bank of America Merrill Lynch, Fischer has also worked for Salomon Brothers and Citi, as well as teaching finance and economics at the University at Albany-SUNY. He has a PhD in Finance from the University of Oregon and a JD from Loyola Law School Los Angeles. He currently lives in New York City.